The
Young Professional's
Guide to

MANAGING

The
Young Professional's
Guide to

MANAGING

Building, Guiding, and Motivating Your Team to Achieve Awesome Results

Aaron McDaniel

author of
The Young Professional's Guide to the Working World

CAREER
PRESS
Pompton Plains, N.J.

THE YOUNG PROFESSIONAL'S GUIDE TO MANAGING
EDITED AND TYPESET BY KARA KUMPEL
Cover design by Howard Grossman/12E Design
Printed in the U.S.A.

To order this title, please call toll-free 1-800-CAREER-1 (NJ and Canada: 201-848-0310) to order using VISA or MasterCard, or for further information on books from Career Press.

The Career Press, Inc.
220 West Parkway, Unit 12
Pompton Plains, NJ 07444
www.careerpress.com

Library of Congress Cataloging-in-Publication Data

McDaniel, Aaron.
    The young professional's guide to managing : building, guiding, and motivating your team to achieve awesome results / by Aaron McDaniel.
        pages cm
    Includes index.
    ISBN 978-1-60163-254-8 (print) -- ISBN 978-1-60163-541-9 (ebook)
    1. Management. 2. Supervision of employees. 3. Employee motivation. 4. Teams in the workplace. I. Title.

HD31.M3829 2013
658.4'022--dc23
                                                              2013007281

To all of the managers I have had in my career: Through your management styles, you have shown me what to do (and not to do) to effectively lead a team. In particular, this book is dedicated to two exemplary managers who reinforce how important having great managers is in building a successful career.

To John Bollinger: You serve as a beacon of consistency, achieving top results no matter the circumstance. You have an uncanny ability to remove obstacles and establish appropriate processes to foster success. You build high-performing teams, and you taught me how to balance competing priorities. You are the best at saying "thank you," showing your employees that they are valued. For all you have done for me let me say, thank *you*.

To Mike Zauner: No one is better at providing employees with the freedom to find their passions while empowering them to accomplish great things. You develop, inspire, and genuinely care about those who work for you. You provide the very definition of how to build trust and most definitely assemble championship teams. Thank you for your endless support and your willingness to take a risk on a "utility player" like me.

Acknowledgments

Although this is the second book in the series it still took a team of dedicated people to make it come to be. It was a bit easier this time around, but there are still so many people I want to thank who contributed along the way.

Thanks to Zach Romano. Your support and guidance continues on. I look forward to working together for years to come. To the rest of the Waterside Productions team, thanks for keeping the wheels in motion for this book series.

To the whole Career Press team. It has continued to be fantastic to work with you. You are all so professional, organized, and flexible (especially when I stretch the rules a bit in my writings). Thank you for always working with me. Michael Pye and Adam Schwartz, you made the transition from Book One to Book Two seamless, and are always creative in finding the best ways to structure my books and solidify the content. Laurie Kelly-Pye, you are so on top of everything, from keeping me in the loop with what's going on to working hard to spread the word about my book. Kirsten Dalley, I couldn't ask for a better developmental editor. Besides being patient and flexible, you set my mind at ease, making me feel comfortable that in the end we will have an awesome finished product. Kara Kumpel, word for word you are the best editor I could ask for. Getting down into the details, you work so hard to make sure my ideas show up well on paper, and you are so good at sending little reminders to keep me moving. Jeff Piasky and Howard Grossman from 12E Designs, I am still loving the silhouette cover design theme. For those that judge a book by its cover, they will think this is one of the best books written on the topic. And last but not least, Gina Talucci, you are such an awesome editorial director, keeping everything on track and helping to make this a fantastic finished product. Thank you all!!!

To Hannah Auerbach and Elise Bogdan from Newman Communications. You both are so phenomenal at what you do. Thank you so much for promoting my books. I feel as though it is almost every day you have another interview for me or a new idea on how to get the word out. I so appreciate your creativity, dedication, and great customer service.

To Jim Kouzes. You inspire me. Thank you so much for believing in this project and in me enough to contribute to it. Your words resonate with me on so many levels. If you think about the sheer volume of things written each day, the fact that your writings (in *The Leadership Challenge* and beyond) are still relevant and sought-after shows the importance of your work and the impact you have on others. I hope that the Millennial generation listens to your sage advice.

Ruth Brandon. Thank you so much for being the best reader I could ever hope for. Combing through pages upon pages of my ramblings and helping polish both the message and the grammar is quite a deed. I am indebted to you and am so blessed that you helped with this project.

Chimmy Lee. You keep rocking it with the great blueprint graphics. They continue to make my ideas much easier to understand.

Paul Benjamin. Thank you for using your lens to capture a picture of me in the best light with my headshot photo. It looks great, as does everything with your artistic touch.

Alexandra Levit, my writing mentor. Thanks for the regular encouragement, reassurance, ideas, and advice. You have paved the way for writers like me.

To AT&T's Leadership Development Program staff, and in particular to Joan Massola and Lizlynne Hannig. You have had such a positive impact on my career. Besides the opportunities your program has provided me as a manager, your support and teachings have been so valuable in my career development. Thank you.

To all the bosses I have ever had. From Tiffany (Hall) Oren, who even at 20 years old showed her amazing leadership and management abilities, providing me with an incredible example of effective leadership (when I was a mere 16 and working at a kids' summer camp), to Marcie Bowerman, Jon Coates, and Alfred Mou, my managers in internship positions, to my bosses through the years at AT&T: Blanca Collins, Robyn (Lee) Moreno, Cecille "Sas" Ruazol, Denise Cunningham, Meryl Graham, John Bollinger, Brian Quinn, and Mike Zauner. Each of you has (in your own way) taught me so much about effective management. Thank you all!

To my friends and family. Thank you for supporting me through the process of writing this book. From those who helped in seemingly small but important ways (like Danny Dardon helping with ideas on how to trim down my book to the proper word count), to all the support I always receive from my parents, Dawn and Jerry, my brother, Marc, and Leona. I am blessed to have you all in my life.

Contents

Foreword
by Jim Kouzes

You Are the Most Important Manager In Your Organization

After reading the manuscript for *The Young Professional's Guide to Managing* I'm reminded of a time not too long ago when I was on a panel at a professional association conference. One of the other panelists was Ken Blanchard, the author of many business books, including *The One-Minute Manager*. In response to an audience member's question, I prefaced my answer by saying, "I don't know what you call something that's been the same for the last 25 years, but..." Before I could finish my sentence, Ken interrupted, exclaiming, "I'd call it the truth!"

Ken's ad lib was both humorous and insightful. He reminded us that some things don't change much over time, if at all, and that we have to understand them for what they are—the *truth*. There are just some fundamentals of leading and managing that are stable through time, even while the context of managing and leading changes dramatically.

That is certainly the case with the lessons Aaron McDaniel teaches in this book. My guess is that if you read this book again 25 years from now, you'll see that what he says here has stood the test of time. His tips are just fundamental to what it takes to manage.

I'd like to underscore Aaron's personal observations with three solid findings from Barry Posner's and my 30 years of leadership research. These are truths that are absolutely essential to understanding the nobility and exercising the power of the managerial role.

The first truth is this: **you make a difference.** It's the most fundamental truth of all. Everything you will ever do as a manager and a leader is based on this truth. Before you can lead others you have to believe that you can have a positive impact on others. Barry and I have been gathering cases from leaders and managers for more than three decades. The people we've talked to come from every type of organization—public and private, government and NGO, high-tech and low-tech, small and large, schools and professional services. They are young and old, male and female, and from every ethnic group. They represent every imaginable vocation and avocation. They reside everywhere around the globe.

And it's not just personal anecdotes we've gathered. We've looked at leader assessments from more than one million people from 74 different countries in the last three years alone. That's a lot of data points. After examining the immense variety of stories from so many different people and places, we can say without hesitation that the most important leader in every organization on the planet is one's immediate manager. It's not the CEO or any other C-Suite executive (unless, of course, you happen to report to one of them). The leader who has the most influence on your desire to stay or leave, your commitment to the organization's vision and values, your ethical decisions and actions, your treatment of customers, your ability to do your job well, and the direction of your career, to name but a few outcomes, is your most immediate manager. And, if you are now a manager, *you are the most important leader to those who report to you.*

So, the question for you is *not* "Do I make a difference?" The question is, "What difference do I want to make?" It's imperative that you spend time answering that question. As a manager, you are offered a profoundly important opportunity to have a positive and lasting impact on the daily lives and long-term successes of all those who are part of your team.

Leadership begins with you and your belief in yourself. Leadership continues only if other people also believe in you. All the courses and classes, all the books and tapes, all the blogs and Websites offering tips and techniques are meaningless unless the people who are supposed to follow believe in the person who's supposed to lead.

The second truth is this: **credibility is the foundation of leadership.** This is the inescapable conclusion we've come to after 30 years of asking people around the world what they look for and admire in a leader, someone whose direction they would *willingly* follow. It turns out that the *believability* of the leader—remember that this is the immediate manager in organizations—determines whether people will willingly give more of their time, talent, energy, experience, intelligence, creativity, and support. Only credible leaders earn commitment, and only commitment builds and regenerates great organizations and communities.

Leadership is a relationship between those who aspire to lead and those who choose to follow. You can't have one without the other. Leadership strategies, tactics, skills, and practices are empty without an understanding of the fundamental dynamics of this relationship. Above all else, people want to believe in their managers. They want to know that you can be trusted, that you have a compelling vision that pulls you and them forward, that you are personally passionate and enthusiastic about the work you are doing, and that you have the necessary knowledge and skill to manage others.

If people are going to willingly follow your direction—and not just comply because you are their manager—it will be because they believe you are credible. To be credible in action, you must do what you say you will do. That means that you must be so clear about your beliefs that you can put them into practice everyday. Consistently living out of values is a behavioral way of demonstrating honesty and trustworthiness. It proves that you believe in the path you have taken and are progressing forward with energy and determination.

The third truth I want to share is perhaps the most important lesson I've learned throughout the years: **you can't do it alone.** No leader or manager ever got anything extraordinary done without the talent and support of others. What strengthens and sustains the relationship between a managers and direct reports—and all the others whom managers depend on—is that great managers are obsessed with what is best for others, not what is best for the manager.

This lesson was driven home more than 30 years ago when we first asked managers to talk about their personal-best leadership experiences. One of the managers we interviewed was Bill Flanagan, then the vice president of manufacturing for Amdahl Corporation. When we asked him to tell us about his personal best, he replied, "I can't." We were quite stunned, and wondered aloud why. Bill said, "Because it wasn't my personal best, it was our personal best. It wasn't me, it was us." We get the same responses today. The best managers—those STARs that Aaron writes about—know in their heart of hearts that they are dependent on the motivation, effort, and commitment of those they manage. They know that it's their job to serve and support those who do the work, day in and day out. In fact, because this truth is so fundamental, we've developed a one-word test to determine if someone has the potential to be a leader and a manager. It's the "we test." When we ask people to tell us their personal-best leadership experiences, we listen not only for the content of the story, but also for the number of times they say "I," and the number of times they say "we." Those who use "we" more often than "I" are significantly more likely to make great managers.

Management is not *about* the manager. It's about the relationship between the manager and his or her team members. Exemplary managers know deep down that they must attend to the needs and aspirations of those they manage if they are going to make extraordinary things happen. You can test this yourself. Just think about a manager you admire and who brought out the best in you—a manager who enabled you to accomplish more than you thought possible. We'll bet that this person believed in you, listened to you, challenged you, developed you, stood by you, and encouraged you. This is the kind of manager we tell stories about later in our lives.

And that person can be you. Because you matter.

Jim Kouzes is the coauthor of the bestselling book *The Leadership Challenge*. He is the Dean's Executive Fellow of Leadership, Leavey School of Business, at Santa Clara University.

You're the Boss Now: What Being a Manager Is *Really* All About

Me: "I need you to keep on working."

Jim: "But boss, it's 10:30 at night and I have been working here since 7am. We are not going to get things to work tonight. I'm tired and want to see my family."

Me: "I'm sorry, but you have to keep working until the customer tells you to go home. We need to focus on getting as many customers in service as possible with this product launch, and every single one counts."

My employee had called me, pleading to let him go home. The job wasn't going to be resolved that night, and regardless how late he stayed he would have to come back the next day. All he wanted was to go home and spend time with his new baby. He had earned it, having worked 15-hour days for seven days straight. It broke my heart to say no, but I had no choice.

Such was life managing a team of new technicians installing and repairing the AT&T U-verse TV service that had just launched. I was managing 30 recently hired technicians in my first job "out in the field."

Contrary to popular manager stereotypes, I didn't *enjoy* forcing someone to work late. Personally, I would have sent everyone home with enough time to rest and be fresh for the next day. Yet I had no such luck. Even when you are the boss, you have a boss of your own to answer to. Unfortunately, being friends with your employees is not the way to exceed expectations.

In the case of these product installations, my boss said that no one was to leave a customer's house unless they either finished the job or were asked to leave by the customer. Today my company has drastically improved the installation process and the customer experience, but at the time we functioned like a start-up and had to fight our way through endless new challenges. It was typical for a job to take 10 hours or more. To meet expectations, I had to push each team member beyond his limits, which I had no pleasure doing.

That night, when Jim finally came back to the garage at midnight, I went out to talk with him. As I walked to his truck I thought, *How am I going to handle this situation?* I had no idea. I had no previous experience to call on. The fact that Jim had only been working for me for a few weeks made my response even more pivotal. We were still building a working relationship that I didn't want to damage.

Instead of giving him a *suck it up* speech or apologizing profusely, I opted for a more direct approach: I gave him the *why* behind having him continue working that night. I assured him that this wasn't meant to be an excuse to abuse our employees, and explained how AT&T had committed to have a certain number of customers in service by the end of the quarter, and we were already behind. I acknowledged his desire to go home and see his family. I told him that I appreciated his hard work, and I committed to giving him a day off in the coming week. I didn't share with him the fact that I had to continue working and prepare a report due that night. I focused on his contribution to the team and confirmed that he was valued, making sure he realized that I understood where he was coming from.

Although I initially had no idea what I was doing, I saw that my actions in the garage motivated Jim and he continued to produce quality work. Later, whenever I really got in a pinch and needed last-minute help with a job, he was there to do it.

It was from this experience that I realized the importance of putting people first, and how this pays dividends through the support and level of hard work your team will give you.

5 Things I Wish I Knew Before Becoming a Manager

1. You have to treat everyone fairly without treating everyone or every situation the same. There is no rulebook that will give you the right answer. Being an effective manager involves a balance of basing decisions on your past experiences, tested principles, and your gut feeling.

2. Being a manager is more than telling people what to do. I used to think that being a manager was going to be easy and fun, but I learned that it can be difficult in many ways.

3. As a manager, you are not only responsible for yourself, your actions, and your results, but also those of each team member. Many times, you are in situations in which you have this responsibility without full control.

4. Your employees may not be able to complete their work as well as you could if you did it on your own. But it is not your job to do their work. Instead, coach them to become better at their jobs while directing them toward attaining team goals.

5. The best individual contributors do not always make the best managers. One of the biggest misconceptions about management is that someone who is good at doing a certain job will be good at managing a team doing that job. Just

because you are the best engineer does not mean you will be the best at managing engineers.

As you forge ahead through an environment of constant change, taking ownership of your career and developing your management style is the best way to be successful. Reading this book is a great step in taking your management acumen to the next level.

Why Read This Book?

Working as an individual-contributor employee does not teach you how to be a successful manager. Being a manager is vastly different from being an individual-contributor employee. You must develop a completely different skill set and become responsible for the actions and results of not only yourself, but also all of the people who work for you.

This book will offer key insights that would take you years to learn on your own. From the basics of transitioning into a management role and effectively facilitating meetings, to empowering others to top results and managing people of different generations, it's all here.

Most importantly, this book is written by a fellow young professional. There are many books about effective management, but none are written *by* a young professional *for* young professionals. Most books on management are written for older generations and are not as relevant for Millennials and less experienced managers. This book offers advice backed by real life experience and is communicated in a way that is easier for us Millennials to understand.

What Will You Get out of Reading This Book?

By reading this book and leveraging the related online resources you will learn:

☆ Basic management skills that are key in transitioning to a management role, such as how to manage both your workload and the demands of running a team.

☆ The 10 skills of successful young managers, including how to drive results through others.

☆ A structured framework to build a plan that encourages your team to consistently perform at a level they did not know was achievable.

☆ How to leverage mentoring and your peers to develop an effective management style.

Who Is This Book For?

This book is for three distinct groups:

1. New or soon-to-be managers who desire to prepare themselves for their new role.

2. People who have managed others for a while and inevitably hit that brick wall of truth: ***managing people is hard***. One observation of Millennials is that we often come into situations thinking, "I got this down," or, "It's going to be easy." With time, we realize that we need to be more proactive about learning how to be an effective manager instead of learning the hard way.

3. More seasoned young managers who are looking to validate their management styles, refine their skills, be reminded of management fundamentals (always a good thing to do), and pick up more easy-to-implement tips along the way.

If you picked up this book and read this far, this book is for you.

Why Me?

As Malcolm Gladwell asserts in his book *Outliers*, it takes 10,000 hours to become truly great at something. I exceeded this threshold in my early career as I managed others in a corporate environment and led teams to consistent, wildly successful results. My experience ranges from operations to sales to customer care, and includes managing employees ranging in the age from younger than me to those more than twice my age. My experience includes managing experienced and new employees, including union workers, in both a structured environment and in ambiguous times of change.

Throughout my short career, I have held a number of management positions and I've managed more than 100 different direct reports in teams as small as two people and as large as 60 (10 of whom also managed others). At AT&T, a Fortune 500 company, I became one of the youngest ever to serve as regional vice president.

That said, there is nothing extraordinary about me or the circumstances I faced. The tips within this book are applicable to every young manager and can be implemented in typical situations you are sure to face.

How to Read This Book

As with the first book in the Young Professional's series (*The Young Professional's Guide to the Working World*), this book accommodates the short attention spans we as Millennials often sustain. Chapters are to the point, and are filled with relevant tips and anecdotes to help you remember the concepts. Also, additional resources online will help you implement strategies to improve your effectiveness as a manager and engage with other young professionals encountering the same challenges.

Throughout the book, you will find the following features:

☆ **"What to Expect"**: At the beginning of each chapter there is a short summary of its main points.

☆ **"Quick Tips"**: These small pieces of simple advice sprinkled throughout the book can often make a big difference.

☆ **"Explore Online"**: The expertise goes beyond these pages to an ever-growing online community that reinvents career mentorship at TheSparkSource.com.

☆ "**The STAR Manager vs. The DOPE Manager**": At the end of each chapter there is a recap contrasting the **DOPE Manager** and the **STAR Manager** as it relates to the topic discussed.

This book will help you succeed upon the first read-through, and will remain a handy resource when you face common management challenges in the future.

A Few Important Things Before We Get Started...

No matter what your title reads or how many people are directly reporting to you, always remember that you are a leader and must take ownership of your development as a manager. Taking yourself seriously as a leader is paramount as a young manager.

Not all leaders are managers, but in order to be effective, managers must also be leaders.

The STAR Manager vs. The DOPE Manager

Just as in the first book in this series, we will look at what you should and should not do through the lens of two opposing archetypes: the STAR manager and the DOPE manager.

The STAR manager is someone who is **S**avvy, **T**enacious, **A**daptive, and **R**esourceful, whereas the DOPE manager is someone who **D**isses **O**pportunity, **P**otential, and **E**arnings. The STAR is someone we aspire to be and DOPE is someone we want to avoid becoming.

A DOPE manager is someone who believes his job is to control his team and ensure that every team member is doing his or her job. While knowing effective ways to motivate or communicate with his team, the DOPE manager tends to take shortcuts because the "right" way to do things is often too hard or time consuming. The DOPE manager gets too wrapped up in his own work to care about the team and focuses on making others do what he thinks is right. When someone on his team struggles, the DOPE manager is less than encouraging, knowing he could do it better himself. He focuses solely on results and selfishly keeps top performers to ensure he always gets the best results. The DOPE's primary goal is to manage his team.

The STAR manager, on the other hand, works to develop her people and supports them in advancing their careers. The STAR manager takes time to provide constructive feedback to those struggling and succeeding alike. She creates a clear vision and continuously motivates employees to achieve top results, fostering a culture of trust, sharing, and teamwork while valuing the creativity her team brings to the table. While the DOPE manager likes feeling superior and in control of his team, the STAR manager surrounds herself with smarter people who fill in her gaps. The STAR manager empowers her employees and recognizes their achievements. The STAR manager both leads *and* manages her team.

As you read through the book, evaluate where you stand on the spectrum of DOPE manager to STAR manager for each topic addressed, and note both the obvious and subtle differences between them. Through the tools available on TheSparkSource.com, you will be able to better understand the areas you excel in (STAR manager attributes) and where you may be struggling (DOPE manager attributes), and then will have the opportunity to create a plan to mitigate your DOPE manager characteristics and turn your STAR manager characteristics into cornerstones of your professional brand.

Finally, **the most important and undeniable truth about your career is that your success in business is more dependent on what you can get *others* to do than what you are capable of doing *yourself*.** Perfecting your ability to lead and manage others is the single most impactful thing you can do.

Managers do things right; leaders do the right thing.
—Warren Bennis

PART I
Management Basics

This first section explores the basic traits managers must develop to effectively run a team. These characteristics provide structure to the second-story addition you are constructing on top of the STAR house you built in Book One, *The Young Professional's Guide to the Working World*.

Before tackling more complex management requirements, such as coaching and motivating a team, one must first learn how to balance the added pressures and responsibilities of being a manager.

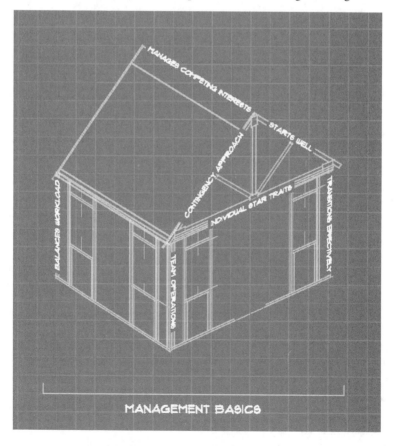

CHAPTER 1

The 25 Attributes of the Successful Young Professional (They Apply to Managers Too!)

What to Expect: The 25 attributes developed by successful young professionals not only support but are closely related to skills needed to be a STAR manager. This chapter covers all 25 attributes of STARs and illustrates their applicability to management roles.

> *A good manager is a man who isn't worried about his own career but rather the careers of those who work for him.*
> —H.S.M. Burnes

Those who have read my first book in the Young Professional's series, *The Young Professional's Guide to the Working World*, are familiar with the 25 attributes of successful young professionals and what sets the STAR apart from the DOPE. For those who haven't read it, I strongly suggest getting a copy of the book, because these attributes are a prerequisite for being an effective manager.

STAR managers know the importance of these attributes in building the foundation for their own careers, and they also know that mastery (or lack of development) of these 25 attributes intensifies when managing a group of people. Not only will gaps in these attributes lead to a toxic team culture and subpar results, but they will also perpetuate bad habits among your employees. As a manager, it is your duty to serve as an example of these attributes and also teach them to your employees—coach them on how to develop into STAR employees, and create a culture where DOPE behavior is not accepted.

In our homebuilding analogy, it is crucial to have a strong ground floor to support the weight of the second floor (management level) you are building. When building a second story, it is important to first reinforce and strengthen the base. Then you must design and build a path (for example, a staircase) that didn't previously exist, connecting your ground floor to the management level being built above. In a sense, when becoming an effective manager, you are re-using and refining the skills and processes you used when building the first story of the house—much the way contractors use similar materials when building the second story on a house.

Here's how your "ground floor" of the 25 attributes of a successful young professional relates to management roles.

Foundational Attributes

1. **A dulled sense of entitlement.** Remember, you don't *deserve* to be manager. Through hard work and circumstance you have *earned* the opportunity to oversee a team. When you transition from individual contributor to manager, you start all over again.

2. **Patience.** You will probably not be an excellent manager from day one. Because you don't have a wealth of experience for reference, there will be many situations in which you will not be sure what to do. Be patient. There is a process to gaining your team's support. Some of your people will get it right away and others won't.

3. **Flexibility.** Each situation is different, and therefore it is important to maintain a flexible management style that can adapt to the circumstances. STAR managers not only need to set the tone by being flexible, but they also have to make sure their employees do not become too attached to the current way things are done.

4. **Learning quickly.** In order to keep your team up to speed in an ever-changing corporate environment, you need to be a step ahead of them. If you are slow to pick up on new trends and best practices, your team will constantly be behind. Encourage your team to ask questions and be patient when you answer them. Otherwise, they will not know how to be effective at their jobs.

5. **Making it about the team.** What your team does will determine whether you are considered a successful manager or a DOPE. Your employees are the ones who actually do the work you are responsible for managing. They are the ones who either reach or fall short of goals. If you put energy into making them successful, you will see better results than if you focus on yourself.

6. **Resilience and follow-through.** As a manager, you are under constant scrutiny and observation by your boss, your peers, and your direct reports. When you give your team a directive, set a specific policy, or commit to a goal, it is essential that you follow through on what you say. Even little things matter. If you commit to your team that you are going to monitor their work but you don't follow up, you will lose credibility and they will know they don't have to listen to you. Never give up on your employees, and follow through with what you say you will do.

7. **Perspective.** Managers need to put all situations in perspective, and they also must translate their perspective to the team. STAR managers are able to take a negative situation and help the team understand why it happened, highlight lessons to be learned, and focus the team on getting past the challenge.

8. **Pride.** Teach your team to take pride in their work. Show them by ensuring your work is of the highest quality, and don't allow them to get by with subpar effort and poor work products. Take things a step further by helping your team understand how what they do is essential to company success.

9. **Self-awareness.** To effectively lead you must first be self-aware. You must understand what you are excelling at and what you struggle with so you can play on your strengths and leverage your team to mitigate your weaknesses, covering your gaps. STAR managers encourage their team to analyze themselves and use resources to discover their strengths and improvement opportunities. Helping your direct reports become self-aware will make coaching easier for you and will increase the possibility that your employees will identify and fix weaknesses on their own.

Quick Tip: Look the part. As a manager, it is important to develop and maintain a sense of professionalism and to serve as a good example to your direct reports. Don't dress down to fit in with your employees; maintain a wardrobe that fits in with office culture but is a step above. Dress for the job that you want, not for the one that you have.

The Frame: Structural Attributes

10. **Customer service.** In addition to your boss and your own (internal or external) customer base, your employees are also

your customers. Find out what they need to be successful, and give it to them. A content employee produces better work. Consistently focus your team on the customers you serve.

11. **Acting "as if."** I have managed teams in multiple functional areas, and in each case had no idea how to do the job that my new employees did when I started. Respect that there will be times when your people know more than you do. Act "as if" you do understand after actively listening to what your people say and observing how they work; they will be your biggest teachers. You must set the tone for your team and act as a leader would act.

12. **Sharp decision-making skills.** As a manager, your team looks to you to make decisions and create direction for them. It is important to weigh the options available and be willing to take appropriate risks. STAR managers take responsibility seriously and think through a decision to find the best path forward. Be willing to make the unpopular decision and stick with it. Effective managers acknowledge when they make the wrong decision. STARs also teach their team to make good decisions through delegation and developing trust.

13. **Creativity.** While a STAR uses her own creativity to produce, a STAR manager also leverages her team's creativity. She realizes that her direct reports have ideas she could never have thought of. Moreover, she recognizes that her people are on the front lines and have a better perspective on creative ways to be successful.

14. **Resourcefulness.** A mistake many newer managers make is thinking that because they are managers, their people are there to do everything for them. The truth is, as a manager you must develop a new set of skills. To build these skills, STAR managers use their people as a resource. Don't be afraid to ask your direct reports for help. They often have the answer, and they like it when you ask, because it shows you value their opinions.

15. **Asking for what you want.** STAR managers sell their people on the vision they create and that they are the best person to lead the team to accomplish this vision. They also sell their boss on the fact that they have a good handle on the team and are guiding them in the right direction.

16. **Taking action.** Managing a team can occasionally be uncomfortable if you are unsure of what you are doing. Be willing to go outside of your comfort zone. The STAR manager learns by doing. She shows confidence even when she is not comfortable and takes appropriate action even in ambiguous situations.

17. **Multitasking.** Managers are forced to juggle their own work as well as ensure that each member of the team is doing his or her job. Managers must also balance their vision with their boss's vision and with what their team wants. Managers play multiple roles. Effective managers are able to seamlessly move from one role to the next while focusing on one thing at a time to ensure quality work.

The Exterior Attributes

18. **Effective communication.** Managers must be careful what they say, because their teams are listening. The STAR manager uses it to her advantage, guiding her team toward success. If you repeatedly talk about one metric the team is measured on, that is all your employees will focus on. The STAR manager also understands the listening side of communication and asks for feedback from her team to improve.

19. **A positive attitude.** Your attitude sets the tone for the team. If you think that a new policy is bad or you feel that a goal is unattainable, your team will follow suit. Be mindful that there are multiple ways to perceive a situation. STAR managers focus on the positive to keep their team focused on goals instead of obstacles.

20. **Having a robust network.** Managers must network for themselves *and* on behalf of their team. Effective managers network to gain support for their team and remove obstacles that are hindering the team's success.

21. **Professionalism.** Professionalism is even more important in a management role because you set the example for the team. If you are too informal or allow your direct reports to get away with something unprofessional, they will continue to act unprofessionally. How your team acts is a direct reflection of you as a manager. Teach your team how to act professionally and find a good mix between formality and informality.

22. **Integrity.** In the same way the STAR is set on her principles but flexible on the path to success, the STAR manager is set on principles and flexible on the management style used to make her team successful. It is important not to tolerate dishonesty or game-playing. Your team will judge you according to how you act in difficult situations, and whether you maintain integrity when opportunities to cut corners arise.

23. **Coachability.** STAR managers know that both their boss and their team will coach them. STAR managers keep an eye out for opportunities to ask their team for advice, but make sure to filter feedback they receive. Different employees will offer diverse coaching points, and managers should only listen to the best advice.

24. **Fostering a culture of giving back.** The STAR manager sets a good example and supports the things that are important to her employees. A culture of giving back must be present in order to empower employees to coach each other and make the team perform better.

25. **Results-orientation.** As with one's own career, results are an important indicator of management effectiveness. The only difference is that it is much harder to get a team to perform

than oneself. At the same time, the scale is bigger. Collective efforts far exceed what a manager could do on her own.

Remember to keep a pulse on these 25 attributes, because you set an example for your direct reports and must take ownership of your own career to continue being a STAR.

It is absurd that a man should rule others, who cannot rule himself.

—Latin proverb

The STAR Manager vs. The DOPE Manager

The DOPE manager sees the transition to management as an opportunity to throw away all that he has previously learned and get others to fill in his weaknesses with their work.

The STAR manager realizes that all the attributes she developed as an individual contributor are even more relevant in a management position, so she labors to maintain these qualities in herself as well as develop them in her employees.

Explore Online: Go to TheSparkSource.com, and click on Resources on the menu bar. Once on the Resources page, find and take the STAR pre-assessment for the **Management Basics** attributes.

CHAPTER 2

Transitioning to Manager: You're Not an Individual Contributor Anymore

What to Expect: Being a manager is much different from being an individual-contributor employee. This chapter addresses the role of the manager. It also discusses the balance between having a "power trip," abusing your authority as a manager, and wanting to be a people pleaser, making sure all your employees are happy. Finally, the chapter notes how managers face intense scrutiny; what they do or say can and will be used against them, or can be inspiring to their employees.

The first responsibility of a leader is to define reality. The last is to say "thank you." In between, the leader is a servant.

—Max DePree

Leadership is the art of getting someone else to do something you want done because he wants to do it.

—Dwight Eisenhower

There I stood, next to a flipchart in front of a conference room, 16 pairs of eyes fixated on me, anticipating my next step and scrutinizing my every move. I felt like a substitute teacher, anxiously waiting for the bell to ring before the class clown could do his best to rattle me.

I felt a heavy sense of responsibility. I was a manager now. And I had no idea what I was doing. Until then, all I had to worry about was my own work, but now I was responsible for the work of 16 other people. I felt like I had just adopted 16 kids.

Although I had prepared somewhat, nothing could have made me ready for what I was doing. On the flip chart, I wrote out our team's goals (which I had learned through a discussion with my new boss) and my expectations for each team member. In the next few minutes, I walked a delicate line, wanting to be seen as an authority figure but not as dictating commands to a group of people who were significantly older than me and also knew how to do their jobs much better than I did.

It didn't go well. Besides receiving combative body language from half the room, I was peppered with questions, each more difficult than the last and every one with an undertone of "Who the heck are *you* to be *my* manager? I don't have to listen to you, and you can't make me do anything." At that moment, I realized being a manager is much harder than it seems on TV.

Throughout the next few months and years, I was able to develop my own management style and learn the basics that all new managers must know to be successful.

Quick Tip: Don't forget what it's like to be an employee. Keeping in perspective how you felt as an employee when certain situations arise will help

you make decisions, and will also help you understand why your employees react in certain ways.

Why Are Managers Important?

Managers, especially mid- and low-level managers, are crucial to
the success of any company. They are able to see what is happening
on the front lines and have the ability to implement (or not implement) strategies that come from above. In *The 360 Degree Leader*,
leadership guru John C. Maxwell asserts that 99 percent of all leadership occurs not from the top but from the middle of an organization.

There are a number of reasons why managers are the most important parts of any organization. Managers are:

☆ **The biggest contributor to job satisfaction.** People often
take a job because of the job itself and leave because of the
manager. A good manager can foster job satisfaction and
career fulfillment for her employees, and a poor manager
can create stress and lead to failure.

☆ **The gatekeeper to a bigger payday.** Managers affect
what people get paid. Managers have great influence over
bonuses and raises.

☆ **The path to career advancement.** Managers are the
first to support or deny any promotion or other career-
advancement opportunity.

☆ **Taskmasters.** Managers dictate who does what work and
when it is due.

As a manager, it is important that you understand the power and
influence you have, and also that you should not abuse the role you
have been given. Young managers must be even more conscious of
this opportunity and must learn to care not only for themselves but
also for their people.

Many people approach the role of a new manager as an opportunity to exert authority. As Linda Hill points out in her *Harvard
Business Review* article "Becoming the Boss," there are a number of
myths about managing people, including:

☆ *Myth: Managers wield significant authority and freedom to make things happen.*
<u>Truth</u>: You won't have more freedom to make things happen; you'll feel constrained by organizational interdependencies.

☆ *Myth: Managers' power derives from their formal position in the company.*
<u>Truth</u>: Power derives from building credibility and trust with your team.

☆ *Myth: Subordinates will obey their manager's orders because of their manager's formal authority over them.*
<u>Truth</u>: Often employees will not obey their manager's directives. How a manager handles authority is what separates the STARs from the DOPEs.

Instead of relying on these mythic expectations, it's important to develop the STAR manager's mindset. To do that, realize these 10 rules to effective management that STARs master and DOPEs never seem to grasp:

1. **It's not about you, it's about the team.** Keep your ego in check. Although you are finally in a position to change some things you dislike about your company, and you finally get to tell people what to do, being a supervisor is a lot more complicated than that. Being a boss is not always glamorous—you have to work hard and pick up the slack if your team doesn't follow through. Remember that being awesome at what you do doesn't necessarily mean you'll be great at managing others. Being an effective manager involves developing a completely separate mindset: **your goal is to make the team successful.** New managers make the mistake of assuming they will be judged on how successful *they* are. In reality, managers are measured according to how well *their team* performs.

2. **Use your power and authority wisely**. Don't go on a power trip. Managers regularly need their people to help them get something done. If you use people as a punching bag, they won't be there for you when you really need them.

3. **Be responsible** for others and for yourself. As a manager, you have additional leverage and scale. When you manage eight people you can harness—or squander—eight times the effort. Good leaders take calculated risks but always consider the responsibility they have for their people.

4. **Watch what you say.** What you focus on and what you say will set the tone for the entire team. Be careful what you say because it will have a direct effect on the work your people do. The same thing can be said for what you do or don't do, so think before you act.

5. **Master the use of control.** STAR managers know when to keep control and when to give it away. Effective leaders offer their team control as a tool to empower better performance. DOPE managers hoard any control they can get.

6. **Be a manager, not a friend.** Many young managers make the mistake of thinking that the more their team likes them, the better they will perform. Your job is *not* to be liked. It's okay that you aren't invited to lunch with your employees. As a new manager, I made this mistake myself, and it was hard to change the way my team perceived me. In later management roles, I felt affirmation when my direct reports would go out for happy hour after work and didn't invite me. It meant I was doing my job.

7. **Follow through.** Anyone can prepare a plan and direct people to accomplish it, but effective managers see plans through to completion. STAR managers guide their team to attain goals and know that if they don't follow through, their team will not follow their lead. Under DOPE managers, employees assume that they don't have to follow orders because there will be no consequences.

8. **Have a plan, but be ready to throw it out.** Planning is an important step as you transition into management positions. It is important to go through the steps of developing a 30-day plan detailing things you want to do, learn, and accomplish. At the same time, be flexible. Circumstances

change, so you must be willing to adapt your plan or throw it out completely and start fresh.

9. **Be okay with not knowing it all.** Transitioning to manager is a profound shift, and you aren't expected to know it all on day one. STAR managers are able to admit when they don't know the answer and aren't afraid to ask for help.

10. **Learn by doing.** Get out of your comfort zone and realize that you have to be the driver for your entire team. As John Candy's character said in *Cool Runnings*, the movie about the 1988 Jamaican Olympic bobsled team, "The driver has to work harder than anyone. He's the first to show up and the last to leave. When his buddies are all out drinking beer, he's up in his room studying pictures of turns."

Although being an effective manager involves developing a new skill set, the attributes you developed in becoming a STAR employee (in *The Young Professional's Guide to the Working World*) become the foundation for your success as a manager. Becoming an effective manager is like building a second-story addition on top of your existing house. Building an additional story on top of your house requires a different process than would a large office building: skyscrapers are built all at once; with your career, you are constantly adding on and improving, piece by piece. You have to plan ahead and build the first story of your house well enough that it can hold the weight of the second. Moreover, there are certain steps you must take, such as applying for permits and obtaining the proper materials, so that the second story matches the ground floor. Then you have to pay for the structure to be built. We will go through the management equivalents of all these steps in this book.

The process of building this second story is divided into two sections:

1. The Basics—These are the beams, flooring, and structure of the second floor, related to the **frame** of the house outlined in Book One.

2. The 10 Attributes of the STAR manager—These represent the walls and roof of the second story, related to the **exterior** of the house from Book One.

As a manager, you fill many roles, including coach, motivator, psychiatrist, teacher, problem solver, innovator, facilitator, change agent, critical thinker, distraction eliminator, detective, translator, filter, and vision setter. As you develop as a manager, is it important to recognize the appropriate moments to play each role. This book will help you understand when and how to fulfill these roles.

During the transition to becoming an effective manager, it's important to remember one of the foundational attributes of successful young professionals: patience. Do not expect to become the best manager overnight. Instead, realize that being an effective leader is a process, as is building the second story on a house. Make sure that you take your time building your management style, and don't forget the importance of having a strong foundation by being a STAR and not a DOPE when it comes to the 25 attributes of a successful young professional (as discussed in the first book of this series).

> *No great manager or leader ever fell from heaven; it's learned, not inherited.*
> —Tom Northup

The STAR Manager vs. The DOPE Manager

The DOPE manager sees being a manager as an opportunity to exert his authority and control what his employees do, expecting that wherever he leads, they will follow.

The STAR manager makes it about the team. All that she does is centered on developing her people and making them successful.

CHAPTER 3

Getting off on the Right Foot:
Success as a Manager
From Day One

What to Expect: Effective management starts on the first day. As a manager, it is important to set the right tone and outline the expectations you have for your team; then go further by communicating these expectations and understanding what your employees' expectations are of you as their manager.

I got even with all the bad management I had by being a good manager.

—Victoria Principal

As the famous Head & Shoulders commercials from the early 1990s remind us, "You never get a second chance to make a first impression." This is true for almost any job, but it is particularly true for management positions. Unless you have built a new team from scratch and have an opportunity to hand-select your direct reports, you are given an already assembled team.

The individuals from the team greet you with either appreciation or disdain, based upon the circumstances before your arrival. They harbor preconceived notions about what you should do to make the team successful. What's worse, they scrutinize your every move. Your people size you up the same way you size them up. Like boxers, they will dance around you and throw quick jabs, testing to see how you react and how much they can get away with. They are analyzing you to see what kind of working relationship they can expect with you, wanting to understand if you are a micro-manager and whether you will be more of a help or a hindrance in getting work done.

Although initial interactions are important and can be intimidating, there is no need to be nervous or to overreact. Despite the propensity for your employees to judge you, it is important to suspend judgment of them. Although the method and style of introducing yourself to the team may vary depending upon your leadership style and circumstance, there is one essential ingredient that allows you to make a solid first impression and begin to build a prosperous team culture: setting expectations.

In college, I taught a student-led course on leadership that was sponsored by the Haas Undergraduate Business School. Each semester I invited Ron Coley, the Associate Vice Chancellor of the university, to speak to the class about his diverse career experiences. One story stood above the rest and provided insight into the one thing all managers must do first when getting a new team. Coley explained that while he was taking a philosophy class in college his professor gave them an assignment to write a paper about the biggest problem in the world. After much thought and reflection, Coley came to the conclusion that it was *mismatched expectations.*

Think about how this has played out in your own life. How many times have you been pleasantly surprised by an unexpected good experience, or upset when things didn't turn out the way you planned?

For example, if you *expected* to receive a 5-percent bonus but received 10 percent you would probably be overjoyed. But if you *anticipated* receiving a 20-percent bonus and received 12 percent, there is a high likelihood you would be upset. Notice that in the second scenario, the raise was higher than the first, but your unhappiness ultimately stemmed from your mismatched expectations.

This is particularly true for expectations you set with your team. STAR managers know that if they don't set clear expectations, either circumstance or team members themselves will create their own expectations of you and what their job will be like. DOPE managers let individuals create their own expectations while STAR managers ensure that every team member has the same set of clear and simple expectations.

> **Quick Tip:** The age question. Because you are a young manager, your employees may look for any reason not to trust you or follow your lead. If they feel as though you are not experienced, they may be resentful that you are in a management position, so it is best not to let them know your age. If they ask, politely let them know that you like to keep that to yourself. Once you have managed for a while and accomplished great things, then you can let them know your age. They will be even more impressed with your maturity and accomplishments.

As leadership guru and author Stephen Covey famously referenced, highly effective people put "first things first." For managers, that first thing is setting expectations. Set expectations during the first very first official team meeting. It may take time for you to understand the scope of the job your team does and its current dynamics, so you don't have to conduct this meeting on day one.

A number of the expectations I typically reference are fairly standard: Be on time, keep an open line of communication and be responsive, have a back-up when you are out of the office, and be accountable. Others are more unique to the particular job. In managing a sales team, I outlined what the sales funnel requirements were along with other system or administrative responsibilities. More expectations would relate to scheduled routines, such as weekly one-on-one status reviews. Others even cover cultural norms, for example, that team members are expected to coach each other.

The purpose is not to overload your people with requirements, so have a strong rationale behind each expectation you set for the team and simplify when possible.

Whereas a DOPE manager may take the conversation this far, the STAR manager understands that expectations are a two-way street: You must also understand the expectations your team has of you. After sharing your expectations, ask for theirs in return. For more experienced employees, this can be refreshing, because most managers they worked for probably never had this kind of conversation. Asking for this information will also help you understand how you can support your team.

Your employees will respond with some standard requests such as this: be accessible or help me when I get stuck with a problem. Other answers will be specific to the job or situation. Once, my team said their number-one expectation was that I guard them from my boss, who previously went behind their old manager's back to talk directly to the team. It's never too late to talk about expectations with your team. Even if you don't have the "expectations talk" when you start managing a team, having it later can be a great way to recalibrate and get the team back on track.

The tone you convey is key. If you come across as condescending or untrusting, you may lose your team for the long haul. **As a general rule, the circumstance should dictate your tone.** Is your new team already performing well, or are they in trouble? Was there an organizational change that caused you to take on a new team, or were some team members passed over for promotion? At times the situation will merit swift and decisive action, and other times it is best to let things continue as is so that you don't disrupt the team's momentum. The way their previous manager ran the team is the largest influencer of the tone you should take.

In one job, I had to lay down the hammer. My new team had been underperforming for quite some time. I could tell that my direct reports had talent, but they had become complacent. Their previous manager let them turn in low-quality work with little consequence.

One particular employee—I will call him Ralph—took the lack of hard work to a new level. His presence was like a cancer within the team. Another employee later told me that the general opinion was, "If Ralph is still working here, I have nothing to worry about. There is *no way* I will get fired, no matter how poorly I do."

My intuition was right, and in response I focused on coaching Ralph to improve, knowing that if he didn't improve and I let him go, the rest of the team would straighten up. And that is exactly what happened. After Ralph was fired, everyone began to refocus on their work, and soon, results improved, so much so that we went from being a mediocre team to being the best in the organization.

> **Quick Tip:** The simple secret to building a great relationship with your people is having good interactions. Most managers only interact with their people when they want something from them. Make an effort to talk with your employees when you don't need anything, just to check in and see how they are doing, or to speak about a topic that is important to them. Your employees will find the interactions refreshing.

The 30-Day Checklist

Besides having a solid first meeting, there are a number of things STAR managers do to ensure that the relationship with their team gets off to a good start. Following are some things to take care of in the first 30 days.

Create a foundation of understanding. STAR managers know that they have managers too, so they seek to understand their boss's goals and make sure their own team goals are aligned. They seek to understand not only how the team is performing compared to other teams, but also the job responsibilities and struggles of their team.

It is also a good idea to understand why the last manager left. Was it because she got a promotion and everyone was sad to see her go? Was it because he wasn't performing well and got demoted?

As I mentioned, it is important to suspend judgment of each of your direct reports. Although I regularly talked to an employee's previous managers, I did not let their opinions cloud my own. Reserving judgment goes a long way toward building relationships with your employees, especially ones who didn't succeed under the last boss but genuinely want to improve.

The first team meeting. At this meeting, in addition to two-way expectation sharing, provide insights into your management style (discussed in Chapter 18) and any goals you have already set for the team. Also, set time aside for your team to ask any questions they have about you, related to your past career experiences or otherwise.

The initial one-on-one meeting. The first one-on-one meeting with each of your direct reports is crucial. This is your chance to obtain individual direct feedback. Many people are not comfortable sharing their thoughts or questions in a big group, so it is important to have these separate conversations. The purpose is to learn more about each of your employees. Don't focus on results; instead, use the time to get to know them. Here are a few important questions to ask:

☆ What motivates you?

☆ How do you prefer to communicate?

☆ How do you like to partner with your manager?

☆ How do you like to be recognized?

☆ What do you like most about your job?

☆ What do you wish you could change about your job?

☆ What are your main strengths and weaknesses?

☆ What do you like to do for fun outside of work?

☆ When is your birthday (without the year)?

☆ How can I, as your manager, help you be successful at doing your job?

☆ What is your favorite candy?

Each question serves a very important point, ranging from seeking to understand how to create a good working relationship, to learning more about them socially, to having them explain what you can do to make them more successful. I typically take note of each answer, and review my notes from time to time, so that I can, for instance, buy each direct report their favorite candy on their birthday. This is a simple example of how to show your employees you care about and listen to them.

Ride days. Ride days, or "shadowing" time, is when you work with one of your direct reports to learn more about his job and observe how he works. These will provide you with various best practices to implement.

Taking time to analyze. Realize that you won't have the answers to every question right away. Like a STAR, be patient and use your resources to understand the major issues within the team and the big opportunities for leaving your mark. It will take time, but this is a step in building team goals and vision. Without this step, a manager might misstep. I have seen executives at my company follow this rule, taking a month or more just to observe new organizations before setting their goals and vision.

Showing you are multifaceted. Remember that your people are human too, so they are okay with you showing a non-authoritative side. It is important to understand the passions of your direct reports (whether you care for those passions or not). If you are able to have a dialogue about something interesting to them, they will be more comfortable around you.

☆ ☆ ☆

By keeping each of these tips in mind, you will be on track to make a solid first impression with your team.

Finally, remember that consistency and follow-through are paramount. Even though you may feel your plan is not working when obstacles appear, be flexible enough to make changes, but stand behind your intuition as well as the plan you put together.

Until all of us have made it, none of us have made it.
—Rosemary Brown

The STAR Manager vs. The DOPE Manager

The DOPE manager jumps into a management position and makes changes that he feels are needed, assuming that the team will support him.

The STAR manager understands the importance of setting accurate expectations and getting off on the right foot with her team, so she puts in extra effort to get to know her employees and make sure they know her.

Explore Online: Worksheets for the first team meeting—Go to TheSparkSource.com Resources page to find the "First Team Meeting" and "First One-on-One Meeting" guides that will help you navigate through the process of transitioning to a new management role.

CHAPTER 4

Workload Balance:
You Can't Always Have an
Open-Door Policy

What to Expect: As a manager, it is important to have an "open door" policy to make your employees comfortable with sharing their thoughts, complaints, and ideas with you, but, if left unmonitored, this policy can create problems as your time becomes monopolized by "drop-bys" and "issues." This chapter details how to balance your own work with your responsibilities as a manager and how to ensure that your employees aren't passing their work off to you.

To do great things is difficult; but to command great things is more difficult.
—Friedrich Nietzsche

55

*One rule of action more important than all others consists
in never doing anything that someone else can do for you.*

—Calvin Coolidge

It had been a productive week. My team was starting to gain some momentum, and I had accomplished a lot, with more to do. When Friday came around, I was ready for the weekend. That morning, I received a few more escalations from my employees and a small assignment from my boss. Right before lunch I looked at my "To Do" list and realized that besides the weekly report I had to put together and the new assignment from my boss, I had nine pending (and urgent) escalations from my team. Half of my team had given me action items, and I realized that I was going to have to work all weekend just to get things done. It was my breaking point.

It became clear that I wasn't pushing my direct reports to solve problems on their own. I was taking on their work instead of teaching them how to do it themselves. Besides wanting to help lighten their workload, I realized that I was focused on making my team like me and think I was better than any of their past managers—a rookie mistake. This caused me a mountain of extra work and gave me employees who weren't empowered to take care of problems independently.

Within a few days, a colleague recommended that I read a book called *The One Minute Manager Meets the Monkey*. In this powerfully simple story, authors Ken Blanchard, William Oncken, and Hal Burrows talk about how inexperienced managers take on their employees' workloads, leaving managers with stress and direct reports without responsibility.

STAR managers know that when managing a team, you must balance your workload and ensure your team is running at optimal performance.

You have reports to fill out, meetings to attend, follow-ups to do, and coaching sessions to complete as you monitor your employees. Each one-on-one session or follow-up you have with a team member is multiplied by the number of people on your team, which makes it more challenging. For example, two or three hours of individual coaching or follow-up with each of your employees adds up to 18 hours of work if you manage a team of six.

As a manager, you wear many hats. Managers must also do their own work, while focusing on the responsibility to direct their team and make sure the team gets its work done. For those desiring to get promoted to middle management and above, it is important to not only have top-performing teams and complete your own administrative work, but also to take on additional projects that impact your organization. You have to excel at not only developing your team members' skills but also your own.

In past roles, I have done everything from running committees to supporting new product launches, to starting new initiatives that I knew would improve the entire organization. As you progress to higher positions within a company, the scope of responsibility, influence, and work gets much broader, so it is important to learn to think at a macro level early in your management career.

DOPE managers let their team dictate how they spend their time. STAR managers proactively balance priorities by gaining control of their time through a simple set of rules.

> **Quick Tip:** Use strategic follow-up to keep your employees on task and completing steps toward accomplishing a task. Set yourself reminders to follow-up periodically, and when you give your employees assignments, let them know when you will be checking in to get status updates. Make sure to follow-through on what you commit to.

The Rules of Effective Workload Balance

1. **Prioritize.** STAR managers are able to balance their work and the responsibilities of managing a team without falling

too far on either extreme. It's a mistake to focus too much on your team's work, yet I have seen even managers at the VP level focus too much on their own work instead of guiding and leading the team. Prioritize your administrative tasks and other responsibilities to ensure your work is completed.

2. **Control the admin work.** When I started working at AT&T, I took an internal training course on time management. One concept really stuck out: The instructor called it "eating your veggies." He explained that although certain to-do list items were hard and not always fun to do (similar to eating vegetables), they were very important and "good for you." A DOPE manager procrastinates on administrative tasks he is responsible for, such as performance reviews, status reports, and managing his inbox. A STAR manager makes sure to budget time to complete some of these items each day.

3. **Create clear ownership of work.** As explained in *The One Minute Manager Meets the Monkey*, much of the workload inexperienced managers take on from their employees stems from not setting a clear path forward when employees come to you with problems. They will come to you asking for help or just explaining an issue they are having. At the end of the conversation, they have a tendency to assume that you will take care of the issue for them. Be clear about who owns each step in solving the problem, and which steps you recommend *they* take. Doing so empowers them to take responsibility. Offer your employees guidance on what to do and explain that if afterward they are still not able to fix the issue, then you will step in to help.

From time to time there will be issues an employee cannot solve his or her own, either because he or she doesn't have authority or because of the urgency of the matter. Strategically taking on a task or two for one of your employees can go a long way in building your relationship. If your team members are stressed or have a number of things they need to get done and you step in to help, they will support you more in the future.

4. **Master the "open door policy."** This term refers to a culture in which people feel comfortable coming to their boss with issues and questions. Whereas I am a big proponent of creating this culture, because it builds trust among your team and helps you understand obstacles so that you can support your team in navigating around them, I also know that there should be limits. A STAR manager makes sure her people know she is approachable, but she also knows that if she doesn't put up any boundaries, then all of her time will be monopolized by drop-bys and questions from her team. She works to avoid distractions, or, at the very least, allows them only on her terms. When she has a deadline or is in the middle of doing her own work, she acknowledges requests and takes a few moments to understand the issue but then explains to her employee that she has to complete something else, and commits to follow up later. This allows you to keep control of your time, and your team will respect you when you show them this courtesy.

5. **Leverage tools.** Many resources are available to help balance your workload. One of the simplest tools is your calendar. Use it to schedule time to complete your work and set reminders to help you keep your team accountable. I am sure a previous boss of mine did this. Whenever he gave me a task, I knew that he would follow up three days later. Because of this, I began to proactively respond to him with a status update before his reminder alerted him to follow up.

6. **Schedule time for yourself.** DOPE managers let their team dictate how they spend their time and have to put in overtime at the office or produce poor-quality work of their own. If you aren't able to complete your own work, then you will find it hard to take on additional responsibility and position yourself for promotion, because you won't have the capacity to take on initiatives that affect the entire organization.

7. **Delegate.** The riskiest, most difficult, and ultimately best way to balance your workload while managing a team is through learning how to properly *delegate*. Delegation is often misused by inexperienced managers. As individual contributors, living in an environment where anything that needs to be done can be done ourselves, we aren't used to having resources that can do work for us. As a manager, you have the ability to assign tasks for your team to do for you. The skill of effective delegation will come into play at various points in this book, so it is important to master it as a foundational skill of managing. Proper delegation and leveraging the unique skills and strengths of each member of your team will help you maximize the limited resources you have to accomplish your goals. Here are some keys to effective delegation:

   ☆ **Delegate to the right person.** Confirm that the direct report you are assigning has the capability, capacity, and interest to complete the task. As Brian Tracy suggests in his book *How the Best Leaders Lead*, match the appropriate individual with each task to maximize overall team productivity.

   ☆ **Explain what you want them to do.** If you expect a certain finished product, describe specifically what you want. The more detail you offer, the closer the finished product will be to what you want. As Mark Samuel puts it, "Delegate to outcomes, not a task." Focus on what end result you expect, not how they go about doing the task.

   ☆ **Confirm they understand what to do and how to do it.** STAR managers take ownership of their communication. Instead of assuming that your direct report grasps what you just explained, confirm understanding.

   ☆ **Let go.** As Sean Connery's character said to Harrison Ford's as he was reaching for the Holy Grail that had fallen down a crevice at the end of the film *Indiana Jones and the Last Crusade,* "Indiana... let it go." Learning to let go is the hardest thing for managers when delegating to employees. Anxiety or distrust is the main reason managers exhibit micro-managing actions. Trust that your team will be able to accomplish the tasks that you delegate to them. It is even more difficult for less-experienced managers to let go because they feel they could do the work better than their employee. —Remember this: *The sum of your team's efforts is much better and bigger than what you can accomplish on your own.* Assume, for example, that your company makes birdhouses. Let's say that on your own you are capable of making 10 birdhouses a day; 12 if you really kill yourself. If you are managing a team of six people who are capable of making eight in each day, is it better to kill yourself to make 12 on your own and focus on increasing your team's output? A STAR manager focuses energy on coaching the team to increase their input from eight to nine each (changing output from 48 to 54) instead of killing herself to make 12 on her own.

☆ **Break the task into pieces.** When delegating, be willing to break a project into pieces and assign parts to multiple members of your team. This way, you can spread out the risk and help improve teaming skills, while still completing the assignment.

☆ **Use it as a development and recognition tool.** Managers can delegate to help develop their employees. Delegating tasks creates great coaching opportunities as well as a way to recognize top performers for their support, while grooming them for promotion and readying them to be successful as managers themselves.

☆ **Follow up and monitor.** A STAR manager inspects what she expects. This does not mean becoming overbearing, but instead adopting former President Ronald Reagan's mentality to *trust but verify*. Ask your employee for status and ask him for feedback throughout the process to ensure he is on track. There is always a chance for you to step in. Be willing to let your employee mess up a little. Delegating offers great coaching opportunities as you help your employees develop through constructive criticism.

☆ **Reward and recognize.** When your employees succeed in accomplishing the tasks you assign, be sure to recognize their efforts. Not only will this improve the quality of work, but it will also make them more willing to help you when you delegate a task in the future. Moreover, be sure to give your employees credit for the work they do when they do help you. It empowers them.

Quick Tip: Manage by walking around. Get out of your office and interact with your people. This is the best way to learn about what obstacles they are facing, the best practices that make them successful, and the general morale of the team. Moreover, it helps you analyze the effectiveness of your management style.

Each of these delegation techniques can improve team results, but remember that you are still ultimately accountable for the finished product. Be sure the work your employees do is up to your standard and that you use delegation effectively to accomplish your goals.

It's not your job to do your people's jobs. It is, however, your job to help them perform at their potential. This takes time, trust, and balancing the work you do, along with overseeing them. Have an open door to be accessible for your people but leverage prioritization and delegation to balance your workload. Maintain control of your time; it's an essential skill of and benefit to the STAR manager.

> *To become truly great, one must stand with the people, not above them.*

—Charles de Montesquieu

The STAR Manager vs. The DOPE Manager

The DOPE manager thinks that, as a manager, he has the authority to get everyone to do everything for him, or he takes on too much of the workload himself, assuming that he can do it better than his team can.

The STAR manager effectively leverages delegation, prioritization, and clear ownership of work to balance her responsibility to oversee her employees with her own administrative duties.

CHAPTER 5

Team Operations:
Effective Meetings and Beyond

What to Expect: The operational side of running a team can be tedious and frustrating (when you are disorganized), or it can be a tool to create momentum and motivation (when mastered). This chapter covers tips on how to run the "back office" operations of your team, from how to hold effective meetings to ensuring proper documentation.

A leader is not an administrator who loves to run others, but someone who carries water for his people so that they can get on with their jobs.

—Robert Townsend

...every time you make a rule you take away a choice, and choice, with all of its illuminating repercussions, is the fuel for learning.

—Marcus Buckingham

"Alright, you went three minutes over your allotted time and used five acronyms that you didn't explain. That's going to cost you $8. Please add it to the penalty pot," proclaimed one of the executives at my company. He was speaking at a leadership planning session a few years ago that, to this day, has remained the most productive meeting I have ever attended. The executive running the division brought together leaders across his organization for the purpose of determining the next year's strategy. As the meeting began, he outlined a set of rules: A timekeeper would be assigned to make sure the entire group stuck to the agenda. If a presenter, including the executive himself, needed more than his allotted time he had to pay $1 per minute. If the timekeeper was off schedule, he had to pay $1 per minute as well. Because corporations are the land of acronyms that not everyone knows, anyone using an acronym before it was explained had to pay another dollar. If someone complained, or laughed at another person's misfortune, there was a $20 fine. By the end of the two-day conference, the jar of money held more than $200 (later donated to charity). Additionally, 50 minutes of each hour were to be dedicated to the meeting, with 10 minutes allocated for checking e-mail, making calls, and using the restroom. This kept everyone fresh and prevented people from being distracted by their smartphones.

Running effective meetings, such as this memorable one, and keeping an organized back office is the management equivalent of the basic "blocking and tackling" in football fundamentals. Whereas a STAR manager may not take it as far as the AT&T executive with the penalty jar, she still understands the importance of effectively using the time she has with her team to communicate important updates and gather the information she needs.

Team Meetings

Team time is sacred time. Outside of this time, your employees are focused on a variety of other things, and it is hard to get their focus and engagement. With my team, I explained that I ask for only one to two hours of their time per week and give them the other 38-plus to do their jobs. That said, I was very protective of that time and focused on making the most of it.

As John C. Maxwell says in *Leadership Gold,* "The secret to a good meeting is the meeting before the meeting." The preparation you put into a meeting is the difference between an effective use of time and a waste. I made an effort to show my team that I respected their time, often spending more than an hour creating an agenda and preparing the content for an hour-long meeting. I would also do my best not to have a meeting for meeting's sake. Each meeting needed to have a set agenda or it would be cut short or cancelled.

Besides setting a solid agenda, here are some more tips, tricks, and advice for holding effective team meetings.

☆ **Have a meeting structure.** The key to structuring your meeting is to know your audience. If you know the team needs a lot of time for discussion or brainstorming, build that into the agenda. If your team easily becomes distracted, work to eliminate any gaps, or build in breaks.

☆ **Create team goal tie-ins.** Regularly referencing team goals and relating them to team updates and organizational changes helps the team focus on the task at hand and prevents them from distraction. When you need to break bad news to your team, relating the news to how it aligns with a team goal cushions the blow.

☆ **Start a "venting session."** As a manager, you learn that people like to complain. Even those who wouldn't complain on their own join the bashing bandwagon when they are in a group environment. Instead of downplaying their pleas or arguing against them, I used a method I call the "venting session." For example, when I managed a group of unionized call center reps, it seemed that they complained about everything! Complaints ranged from the heat and lighting in the building, to lunch break times and policies they thought were stupid. To combat these complaints, I set aside time during our weekly team meeting to talk about such issues: the "venting session." During the first venting session, the complaining lasted nearly an hour. Instead of making excuses, I took out a pen and paper and wrote down all the concerns they voiced, occasionally asking them a question to clarify that I understood the issue. After each meeting, I went and found out as much about the issue as possible. There were times when there was nothing I could do, and other times I worked to get the answer they needed or fix a process to make their job easier. In time, something amazing happened: venting sessions decreased from 45 minutes to 15 minutes, and then to five minutes; about five months later, everyone sat contently, saying, "We have nothing to talk about. I think we're good." Besides helping me understand the issues I could eliminate, this did wonders for building trust and earned me enthusiastic support from my team.

☆ **Educate your team.** Team time is also learning time. During each meeting, find ways to teach something new to your direct reports. It is important to keep learning. At times, I quiz my team on new concepts they should understand, which allows me to both monitor their development and teach them something new. I have also had teams in which we read a book, break coursework into pieces, or study a framework together. Not only is this relevant to our jobs, but it also builds a culture of helping and teaching each other.

☆ **Bring in the outside world.** It's easy for people to get lost in the day-to-day, completely focused on their specific job responsibilities. It is our job to help our people understand not only how their role is important to the company, but also what is going on outside the organization. One way to do this is through helping the team understand the reasoning behind certain policies. For example, when I was a sales manager, my salespeople often became upset that they didn't get paid for selling certain products in our portfolio. It was my job to help them understand that there was another organization focused on selling that product, and although some of my people's customers might need the product, the company designed the organizational structure in a specific way, and didn't pay them on that product for a reason. Another way I tie in the outside world is by setting aside time for industry news during each meeting. While preparing for each meeting, I spend time compiling news stories that may not affect our jobs but do relate to our company or customers. This took time and discipline to do regularly, but it became my team's favorite part of each meeting.

☆ **Delegate to develop.** STAR managers use team time to develop their people. Instead of making it solely a time to talk *at* people, a STAR manager actively engages her employees by delegating responsibility for parts of the meeting to them. Instead of teaching the team about a technique to do their job better, have one of your employees research it and present it to the team. It improves his skills and saves you some time. The educational elements of a meeting are a great time to delegate and engage your team members.

☆ **Recognize accomplishments.** Team time is a great opportunity to recognize the accomplishments of your people. Team recognition will be addressed more thoroughly later in the book, but for now, one simple way to recognize your team is through "shout-outs." At the end of each team meeting, I set time aside for people to thank each other by giving them a "shout-out." Shout-outs don't come with any prize or certificate; they are just words, but they are an effective teambuilding tool. Shout-outs can range from making the team aware of a best practice that a peer discovered, to a chance for team members to thank each other for a ride from the airport or helping fix a work problem. Shout-outs are also a great way for you to reinforce good behavior and let each person on the team know he or she is appreciated. Don't be too liberal with shout-outs so that they keep a high value, and be prepared to start off the "shout-out"-giving. Very soon the team will embrace the concept, giving their own shout-outs.

> **Quick Tip:** Maintain a document that keeps a running record of all notable events and incidents involving your employees. This will help you coach your employees to improve and will be a valuable repository of evidence if you must take disciplinary action against one of your employees.

Documentation

Whereas team meetings are an important part of maintaining effective team operations, documentation helps you keep your people in line. Documentation is probably the most tedious and annoying part of being a manager, but it is crucial to your success.

DOPE managers may keep a mental tabulation of all the things their people do, believing that they can call on these situations during coaching sessions or when they need to fire someone, but the STAR actively takes notes that she refers to when needed.

I keep a running list of things my people do. It might be a mistake made, a situation in which someone didn't act professionally, or a time when someone turned in a poor work product. This is not a list of ills to use as blackmail against them, but you will be able to back up your decisions when you have facts and specific examples of issues for your employees. Documentation becomes especially important when you have a poorly performing employee whom you need to put on a performance improvement plan.

Here are five quick tips to ensure proper documentation.

1. **Be detailed.** Keep a record of times, dates, parties involved, and other relevant facts.

2. **Write it out like a conversation.** Some documentation is a quick observation, but other times it is an interaction. If you can, write the dialogue you have as if you are writing a movie script. Include both what they say and what you say.

3. **Save e-mails.** Effectively documenting is not just about writing out notes; it's about saving evidence. E-mail is an amazing way to keep track of interactions you had with employees, and it provides insight into the sequence in which things happened. Save your Sent folder to help with this.

4. **Record it right away.** Don't wait two weeks—or even until the end of the current week—to document a situation. Record your notes immediately.

5. **Be honest.** Make an effort to be accurate with your notes. Don't leave anything out, even if it involves you making a mistake. When you have an employee on a formal performance plan, you may be expected to share documentation with them, and you don't want to get caught being inaccurate confirm that you were being accurate.

Effective Rules and Processes

Through trial and error, I have developed additional methods of team management that come in handy when my team falls short of expectations. With one team, I dealt with both a tardiness issue and a lack of attention to detail with the expense reports and recording results. In response, I devised the "Team Contribution Fund." For each mistake made by an employee, he had the "opportunity" to donate to the fund. Although I couldn't make it mandatory, I fine my employees $1 for every time they were late to a meeting or call, $5 for every time they submitted an incorrect report, and $25 if they ever miss a meeting and didn't let me know ahead of time. Periodically, I use the money for a team recognition event. In response, everyone began to come to meetings on time and I rarely had to send back incorrect reports.

Another effective method for keeping your team organized and focused is to send out a summary e-mail each week with all the information your team needs to know. Employees are bombarded with e-mails—updates from organization leaders, corporate programs, and new systems, plus messages from customers, and so on—much of which are a waste of time. Help your team know what is important by summarizing all the most pertinent information and then review it with them during team meetings. I marketed this summary e-mail as the *one* message my employees should completely read each week. To ensure that everyone was actually reading it, I tested the team periodically. Every once in a while I attached an e-mail (among other attachments) that said something like, "If you are the first person to reply back to this e-mail with the word TEAM in capital letters, I will buy you lunch." I had to buy lunch from time to time, but it also showed me who was reading and who wasn't.

Effective team operations are a continuous process that takes time and conscious effort. Despite the hard work, accepting this challenge allows you to show your creativity. You may not need to invent a monetary penalty system or a grand team meeting agenda in which everything is planned down to the minute, but these efforts will help you keep your team under control instead of spinning into chaos.

What you cannot enforce, do not command.

—Sophocles

The STAR Manager vs. The DOPE Manager

The DOPE manager ineffectively uses team time, does not rely on set processes to stay organized, and sets either too many rules that stifle employee morale, or too few rules, causing the team to scatter in many directions.

The STAR manager develops clear processes and norms to help her team run more efficiently. She is organized, makes the most of team time, and makes effective use of documentation and appropriate team rules.

CHAPTER 6

Caught in the Middle: Managing the Competing Interests of Your Boss and Your Team

What to Expect: Experienced managers know that they serve two masters: their boss and their people. The goals, focus, and desires of the team you manage will inevitably clash with the directives you receive directly from your boss and upper management. This chapter discusses effective techniques that allow young managers to walk the line between keeping their employees happy and keeping the boss satisfied.

You can get everything in life you want if you will just help other people get what they want!

—Zig Ziglar

Make your top managers rich and they will make you rich.
—Robert H. Johnson

"I have big news, everyone!" I exclaimed as I started the weekly meeting with my small business sales team. "We have a new small business bundle of products that allows us to sell a bunch of new products that are perfect for our market segment. Plus," I added to sell the point with a big finish, "for these bundles we will get three times the commission over the next three months!"

I waited for cheers of excitement, but all I got back were blank stares. "What do you guys think?" I inquired. Then the silence was broken and the complaints gushed out.

"Great, I bet now our quota is going to increase because of this bundle," one of my people stated.

"You know how this works; the first few sales are always a NIGHTMARE! System problems, part of the process that the product designers forgot to include... Last time I almost took one of my customers out of business with the issues," a top performer explained.

One last person joined in: "Can you at least ask our VP to give us some time to actually get trained on the product set before requiring that we sell it?"

In response to this barrage, all I could say was, "Well, I understand there will be issues, but our organization's leadership put millions of dollars into developing this platform and we are getting a directive from our VP that we have to start selling this." Not the best response I have given when under attack, and only a small step up from the age-old "because I said so" reply. Leaving that meeting I could tell that my team felt that I wasn't standing up for them.

As a manager, you are often stuck between a rock and a hard place; between supporting your team and following your boss's lead. In fact, this is one of the hardest foundational attributes to develop, and one that you must constantly refine as new and unique situations continuously arise.

Your employees will always want less work, more freedom, and autonomy to do what they need to do, with few processes or procedures to occupy their time. Simultaneously, your boss will want consistent, solid results and unquestioned support whenever she introduces a new idea or asks you to do something new and different.

Author John C. Maxwell, in his book *The 360° Leader*, astutely breaks these competing responsibilities into three categories:

1. **Lead-Up:** This includes supporting your boss, while knowing when to push her to change and when to back off and accept her direction.

2. **Lead-Across:** In this role you help your peers achieve results, develop a respectful working relationship, and gain credibility for when you need help.

3. **Lead-Down:** This is when you focus on your people, serving as a model and guiding them to reach their potential and achieve goals.

Now let's discuss how to manage your boss, employees, and peers simultaneously—and successfully. In doing so, you play four distinct roles: the *filter*, the *translator*, the *advocate*, and the *negotiator*.

The Filter

As a manager, you are often the central communication point; a filter for both your boss and your people, using your decision-making skills to give your boss affirmation and alignment while giving your people direction.

In the filter role, it is important to take ownership of what you communicate to your team, unlike what I did during the situation shared at the beginning of this chapter. Similarly, I once had a boss who was a terrible filter. During weekly meetings, he would reference his boss more than a dozen times. "Todd wants us to do this." "Todd asked me to do that." "We don't want to get in trouble with Todd, so we better fix this issue."

The result was that our team was not inspired to support our boss. He was just a pushover who wanted to stay out of trouble. His spineless mentality assured us that he would never filter any bad news and wouldn't fight for us to fix a bad policy or right a wrong decision.

The STAR manager takes ownership of what she communicates and makes it appear to her team not only that directives are coming from her, but that she and her boss form a unified front, even when she disagrees.

As a filter, STAR managers limit the information they share with their team and with their boss. If your boss gets angry about something your team did, that doesn't mean you need to bark the same message at your team. Instead, find the few key points to get across and change your style to motivate your team.

> **Quick Tip:** Don't be the scapegoat or have a scapegoat of your own. Some bosses constantly, publicly pick on a certain person on the team. It may be because of his poor performance or inability to effectively communicate with his boss. Ensure that you are not the scapegoat used as an example on your leadership team, and don't single out a scapegoat on your team.

The Translator

Just because your boss shares an organizational update or gives you an assignment does not mean that you need to share the same message verbatim with your team. In many ways, your boss and team speak separate languages, and you are the interpreter between them.

A justifiable reason for poor results heard from your team may come across as an excuse if you communicate it in the same words to your boss. It's important to add facts and evidence to what you communicate. As a manager, you have the benefit of getting visibility into the experience of your entire team, not just your own experience. This means that, with five employees, you have five times the experience to use that will help you translate the message and tie in supporting evidence. This also allows you to better align the news you share with your team (or the excuses for lack of performance you tell your boss) with the boss's goals.

For example, if your boss likes to hear about actions you plan to take when your team is not meeting expectations, translate the message into a language he can understand by weaving the issues your team faces into an action plan you are initiating to improve results.

The Advocate

A manager is a lot like a politician who has to toggle between supporting constituents and supporting the leaders of his party. You must be an advocate for your people but also support the goals and vision set by your boss. Just like a politician, you must be the voice of your people with your boss. If your team insists that a new job requirement isn't fair, it is important for you to share this message with your boss.

STAR managers are also advocates for their boss by selling their direct reports on why everyone should buy into the organization's goals and focus.

Finally, STAR managers are an advocate for their boss by helping to mitigate his gaps. If your boss is weak in a certain area, such as rewarding good performance, mask this shortcoming by finding ways to partner with your boss to celebrate the success of your people. For example, write a congratulatory letter on behalf of your boss recognizing an achievement of one of your direct reports and ask him to sign it.

DOPE managers don't realize how important it is to stand up for their team. Effective managers are willing to say no to their boss when they feel what he is doing will hurt their team. While it is important to pick your battles, when your boss crosses the line, you are your team's only defense. There will be times when your boss may incorrectly accuse your team of doing something wrong or may miss something significant they accomplished. You must be the one to set the record straight. When you successfully stick up for them, your team will support you and work even harder to help you reach the goals you set. Moreover, your boss will respect you for supporting your people.

The Negotiator

After you learn how to say no to your boss in the advocate role, it is important to find a common ground that will work for both your boss and your people. Otherwise, when you fight your boss or demand something of your team, you lose the support of both sides. Think of some compromises. The DOPE manager can uncover issues, but the STAR manager jumps into action like the Priceline Negotiator to find lasting solutions that both her boss and team buy in to.

When leading a sales team, I required that all salespeople update a Customer Relations Management (CRM) system daily. Naturally arduous requirements like daily system updates became taxing for my team and generated complaints from my boss when my people did not meet expectations. Instead of demanding that my team follow these strict and conflicting guidelines or admitting to my boss that I couldn't get them to comply, I found a common ground.

I asked my team what they felt were a reasonable number of times they should update the CRM system. They felt once a week was fair, given the amount of time it took to update. I talked to my boss and learned that there were two times a week when he needed to know current CRM activities from my team to report to his boss. I negotiated with him and we agreed that twice a week, the day before the readouts, I would ensure that my team had updated the CRM system. In the end, both my boss and team were satisfied.

Even as a Manager, You Are Still on a Team

Just because you are the boss does not mean you no longer serve on a team of your own. The team you are a part of becomes much more complex when your peers are managing people instead of just being individual contributors. Each leadership team has its own dynamics, but when you realize that ultimately you all have the same goal of leading your teams to great results and supporting them however you can, you will see that you are no better or worse than they are. Thoough your peers can cause you frustration, they are also one of the best resources available to help you manage your team.

Here are a couple ways that your peers can become a challenge to managing your team:

☆ **Competing interests.** At times you and your peers will have competing interests. Generally, managers want their team to do best and will do what it takes to ensure this. Once, a peer of mine misled me to believe that someone on his team who was moving to my geographic area would be a good team member for me. Despite past issues, my peer assured me that this employee had drastically improved. In reality, this employee had not improved and was soon a poison to the culture of my existing top-performing team. It took a great deal of failed coaching and administrative work to fire him almost eight months later.

☆ **Challenge to your authority.** Each manager runs her team in a certain way, with her own unique style. When one of my peers has a different policy on something, I tend to hear about it from my direct reports. "But Jan doesn't make her team do that," they lament. Despite how these differences challenge your authority, stay firm with the style you feel is right.

If you choose to be an island, isolated from interaction and collaboration with your peers, then you are actually stunting the growth of your team and preventing them from reaching their potential.

Despite these challenges, there are many advantages to building a strong relationship with your peers, including:

☆ **Best practices.** Some of the greatest resources for what to do or not do in managing a team are your peers. DOPE managers focus solely on their team and what they feel is the right way to manage, while the STAR manager keeps an eye on her peers to understand the best methods to motivate and manage a team.

☆ **An extra set of eyes.** Your peers see things, both good and bad, that your team does. Your peers can help you understand whether your employees are really doing their job and can alert you when someone needs to be coached. It is important to offer this same support to your peers by being the eyes and ears for them and sharing potential coaching opportunities for their employees.

☆ **A sounding board.** Your peers are great resources off of which to bounce new ideas. They can provide feedback on similar strategies they have used and can tell you what worked for them and why. Their different viewpoint on leadership is a great resource to help you refine your own style and management tactics. Ensure that you are the same sounding board for them as well.

☆ **Backup.** Whereas I think it's a good idea to let the top performers you are grooming for promotion back you up when you are out of the office, it is also smart to have a peer backup as well. There will be certain approvals that your peer backup can give that your employee cannot.

☆ **Competition to perform better.** I have frequently found that it is much easier to motivate a team to perform well when they are competing against another team and not just against a goal. While a DOPE manager allows competition to become personal, it is important to aim for friendly competition and ensure that you are still partnering with their peers and other teams.

☆ **Mentors for your people.** As you seek to develop your people for promotion, it is often effective to assign them a mentor other than yourself. Your peers can be a huge help in mentoring your top performers.

☆ **Partners.** When I was a call center manager, I regularly partnered with a peer to put on joint initiatives. Not only could we leverage each other as resources, sharing the responsibility of facilitating the initiative, but we were also able to make our ideas better by pooling our creativity. STAR managers see their peers as partners and regularly work together to make both teams better.

STAR managers avoid the politics that often arise when being a part of a leadership team, and instead focus on supporting their peers' goals and leveraging them to help their team perform even better.

Overall, the thing that STAR managers keep in mind when partnering with peers and serving as a filter, translator, advocate, and negotiator is that successfully managing up, down, and laterally takes patience. It's natural to want quick results or abandon building a relationship if there aren't immediate benefits. I urge all young professionals to be patient as they develop relationships with bosses, teams, and peers; collectively these three groups (and the ability to manage and satisfy all of them at once) are what make STAR managers consistently successful.

> *Leadership is a two-way street, loyalty up and loyalty down. Respect for one's superiors; care for one's crew.*
> —Grace Hopper

The STAR Manager vs. The DOPE Manager

The DOPE manager either blindly follows his boss's guidance or actively rebels, only doing what his employees want to do. He competes against his peers and is not open about sharing best practices with his leadership team.

The STAR manager is an advocate for her team while accurately supporting her boss's agenda and goals. She is a contributing member of her leadership team and partners with her peers to both help them and more effectively manage her own team.

CHAPTER 7
It Depends:
The Contingency Approach to Management

What to Expect: Not every situation is the same. Managers who stick to only one set plan or set of rules will fail, but so will those who make too many exceptions. This chapter explores the benefits of the contingency approach to management, treating each situation as a chance to use a fresh set of eyes to make the appropriate decision, and doing so with integrity and consistency.

Fit no stereotypes. Don't chase the latest management fads. The situation dictates which approach best accomplishes the team's mission.

—Colin Powell

"You're five minutes late coming back from your break again," I said, annoyed at having to discipline an employee for the same issue more than once.

"So what? It's only five minutes. I had to go to the bathroom and take care of a few things," Tina snapped back.

Normally I cut my employees a little slack here and there, but Tina had taken things too far. She was a classic case: treat her special and she was a pleasant employee, but hold her to the same rules and standards as everyone else and you were in for a fight.

After multiple coaching sessions and disregarded commitments for a number of other issues, it was time to take action. I knew she was going to be late on purpose. She had tested me for the last week and finally it was time to act. After her response, I called her into the conference room to give her a formal suspension and warning of dismissal.

Walking a few paces ahead of her, I reached the conference room and began to sit down. I was dumbfounded to see that just as she was about to reach the conference room door she turned and stormed into my boss's office. After Tina admitted she was late, my boss defended me, leading Tina to claim she had a migraine headache, referencing the Family Medical Leave Act (FMLA), something that by law we couldn't question her about. Tina then proceeded to stay out on "disability" until I moved on to a new job a few months later. She returned to work literally the day after I left.

Not long after this altercation, another employee was late coming back from break. It was the second time that week but she had recently found out a close family member had died and was spending her breaks making funeral arrangements outside in the parking lot. My heart went out to her, and despite these missteps, she was a consistent hard worker who delivered quality results. I decided to let her slide a bit.

Though these may not be typical situations all managers will encounter, but they are characteristic of the types of challenges you will face while managing a team of diverse personalities in a variety of situations. I learned a valuable lesson about effective management from these situations:

> *STAR managers understand that although each situation they face is unique and should be treated accordingly, it is important to remain consistent in upholding their principles and fair in enforcing their rules.*

Just as a STAR individual contributor is firm in her integrity but flexible on her path to success, a STAR manager must look at each situation and evaluate it according the facts, established principles, and past actions.

Managers must walk the line between complete and consistent fairness and targeted deviations, depending on the person and situation. If, for example, your top performer makes a minor mistake on an insignificant task, your response should be different than if a poor performer who consistently and carelessly messes up makes the same mistake. This is where management becomes an art.

The science comes into play when you have to look at your track record through time and stand behind your decisions, tying your action to some kind of standard or benchmark. A STAR manager masters this art and science.

I refer to this type of "it depends" mentality as a **contingency approach to management**. Through effective utilization of the contingency approach, you have a higher likelihood of success as a manager no matter what business function you work in, what company you work for, or what industry you are a part of. When considering the best choice to take under the contingency approach, four main factors will affect your decision: the situation, the employee(s) involved, the principles you have established for your team, and your track record of decision-making in similar situations. For the sake of this analysis, we fill focus more on the situational and employee-related factors, noting that whereas the others are important, they are more intuitive (and were addressed in Book One).

The Situation

The most dynamic managers can get employees to produce great results no matter the situation; however, particularly at the executive level, managers tend to become experts at leading a team through one certain type of situation. A STAR manager is able to leverage the contingency approach to lead her team to success no matter what the circumstance.

Here is a breakdown of five different situations and how to best respond. Keep in mind that there will be times when multiple situations occur at once and you must combine strategies in order to succeed.

1. **Cleanup.** In these situations, managers must stop the bleeding by focusing on eliminating the individuals and processes that hinder the team from reaching their potential, and keeping the things that are good. Although it may take a significant amount of restructuring, plug the leak, and then focus on moving to the turn-around stage.

2. **Turn-arounds.** STAR managers come in to turn-around scenarios realizing that many times the issue lies in generally accepted norms and a sub-optimal culture. Establish new rules and make decisions that support a new way of doing things instead of old, comfortable practices. Realize that you may encounter pushback, because many employees may not recognize that it is time for a turn-around.

3. **Keeping momentum.** There will be times when you are given a team that is working well with solid results. A DOPE manager feels the need to exert his power, purposely changing things that are working. Instead, do your best to get out of the way and focus on removing obstacles so that the team performs even better than before.

4. **Shifting focus.** As a manager, you will face situations in which you will need to support your team in adapting to strive for a new set of goals or temporary circumstance. STAR managers realize that these situations, especially when

they affect a team that is performing well, are unsettling for employees, and it is important to help the team see where previous best practices are still applicable and where flexibility is needed.

5. **Building/starting.** Besides the focus on bringing in appropriate talent and setting norms, a STAR manager allows her people to experiment to find the best way to do things in uncharted territory. She encourages risk-taking but guides the team away from clear failures.

Generally the best way to determine what situation you are in is to look at the results of the team you are managing as they relate to the organization's goals. If the organization is doing well, your role will be more focused on building momentum, as opposed to right after an organizational change when there is a shift in focus and it is possibly a time to start anew and build toward a new set of goals.

The Person

The people factor is often what most affects the approach you take and the decision you make. The litmus test you run through, however, is not as simple as a determination of whether your employee is a low, medium, or high performer. The following are 14 different types of people and suggestions on the best way to manage each. As previously mentioned in the outlining of each situation, most people will be a combination of a few of these types rather than just one, and there may be variations of people not specifically addressed in the types outlined.

Warning: Don't make snap judgments about your people according to the types outlined here. Additionally, don't use these types as a justification to dislike or stereotype someone. In time, people will change, either through your coaching or on their own; for example, a "high flyer" can transition to a "has been."

1. **High flyers.** High flyers are top performers who consistently perform at the highest level. They tend to fall into two categories: they are either (A) selfish types who want

special treatment as recognition for their top results, or (B) team players who understand their power within the group, choosing to support your management style and initiatives. It is best to reward type B people with added responsibility and recognition, and in type A's case to remind them that they still need to play by the same rules as everyone else.

2. **Roller-coaster riders.** This type is consistently inconsistent. I have had employees who are generally mediocre until I put them on a coaching plan; they perform well until they meet the expectations of the plan, and then proceed to let their results drop again. A STAR manager uncovers the true root of the inconsistency and continuously monitors the roller-coaster riders to ensure they don't have the opportunity to drop below expectations.

3. **Budding managers.** There is usually at least someone on most teams who has what it takes to become a manager. Whether they have past leadership experience or good self-awareness, they tend to have a better understanding of the struggles of being a manager and so they work to support you with their peers. It is best to recognize this type and regularly pull them aside to give them the inside scoop. This includes sharing with them why you made a certain decision, and asking their opinion when you are faced with a decision.

4. **Has-beens.** This flavor of employee was once at the top but has fallen from grace. Typically, they tend to still feel that they deserve to be treated like a top performer, including receiving special treatment from their manager. Reasons for the decline can range from boredom with a position to inflexibility in the face of change. The best approach is to uncover why there has been a decline in performance and motivate them to return to top results by offering them rewards (such as more freedoms) once they return to consistent, solid results. If they are not able to improve, help them find a new position that is a better fit for their skills, remembering and respecting the top results they once produced.

5. **Aspiring friends.** These employees believe they are your friend and not your employee. They will test every angle, being friendly with hopes that it will gain them more freedom later. It is important to be forthcoming and direct that they are *not* your friend and that they work for you. Despite their efforts to befriend or influence you, don't fall into an informal relationship. Retain your principles and manage them by the book, because the moment you begin making exceptions, the harder they will push until you have little authority over them.

6. **Gossips.** The office gossip always has a story to tell. Whether it is with you or with coworkers, they are grand distracters. Besides quelling their politicking, put any issue they bring to you through a filter. I have had employees in the past come to me claiming that "everyone" has a problem with a certain process or decision I made, when in reality there were only two people with an issue.

7. **Contrarians.** There are arguers among us; people who will disagree with the group and potentially fight against your initiatives that the rest of your team accepts. Instead of fighting back, channel this dissent and leverage it to validate your decisions. Specifically ask their opinion and show that it is valued. Contrarians can often uncover issues you and the rest of the team overlook. Despite the annoyance, they can be a valuable resource that makes your ideas even better.

8. **Outsiders.** Whereas most people like to develop relationships with their coworkers, regularly interacting with them informally, if not socially, the outsider likes to keep to herself. She stays out of office politics and is generally less vocal about her opinion, because of bad past experiences or an inability to relate to others on the team. It is best to find ways to pull out her opinions, because they can be good ones. Often these will come in private, as opposed to in front of the group.

9. **Social directors.** To social directors, work is about having fun. They may be good at focusing on their work when

needed but have a propensity to get distracted by things they are planning outside of work. They also tend to be the glue that holds the team together socially. Although they can be a distraction, leverage their social skills to rally the team around your initiatives.

10. **Swing people.** Swing people tend not to be opinionated and can change their support or dissent of an idea instantaneously. A friend of mine is an attorney who focuses on jury selection and admits that they look for a number of swing people they can influence when choosing the most advantageous jury. Use these swing people to your advantage, supporting you as a manager, especially in times when you seek consensus from the team.

11. **Debbie Downers.** According to Debbie Downers, the sky is always falling. These employees are complainers at their core and will always look for the negative. It is important to not let their ill-feelings poison the team. Make an effort to downplay their challenges and look for ways to privately coach them to look for the positive.

12. **Hand holders.** These employees must get detail, specific direction, and permission to take any action. They want you to make their decisions, so they don't have any accountability. Don't let hand holders get away with not being accountable, and openly require them to make decisions so they become more comfortable with it, leading them to become more proactive.

13. **Yes men.** The yes man always seems to agree with you. No matter what you say, he appears to be on board. However, below the surface he may have different beliefs. Get to the core of where he stands in regular one-on-one reviews and encourage him to share his true opinions. Focus on how he really *feels* more than what he *says*.

14. **Talkers.** Talkers talk a big game but have no follow-through. They seem as though they understand you and are in the process of getting work done, but the results don't follow.

With this type of employee, hold them to their commitments and swiftly move toward formal coaching if they don't. Focus on results more than talk.

The best way to determine employees' combinations is by looking at their results and, more importantly, observing how they interact with both you and their peers. Generally these consistent behaviors will shed light on the best general management approach to take with each type. Remember, however, that the overarching situation, as well as a more specific circumstance, such as an employee's poor performance related to an external factor, should be taken into consideration.

Circumstances, situations, people, performance, and track record aside, there is one high-level rule to keep in mind, which I refer to as the ***Platinum Rule of Contingency***. This rule is:

> *Lead in such a way that if the rest of the team and your boss found out how you've made a decision or managed a situation, they would be fine with it and feel that it is consistent with how you should act as a manager.*

In making a decision, you also want to vary your management style along the spectrum of autocratic, consensus-based, and even majority-rules decision-making. STAR managers are able to evaluate the right time to use each style, depending on both the situation and people involved. Here is some insight on when to use each style:

- **Autocratic.** When quick decisions need to be made, or decisions you know will be unpopular but necessary, autocratic decisions make sense. Use this style when you are very passionate or sure about a certain path forward, despite how your people respond.

- **Consensus.** It is a good management practice to periodically include your employees in the decision-making process. This is especially effective with decisions that have a big impact on your team or that you need specific effort or support for.

- **Democratic.** This is a natural method for us to use, but we must be careful not to alienate employees just because they are in the minority. If they are of the contrarian or outsider type, this may alienate them from the group.

Without the contingency approach and adaptive management techniques, you will fail and will learn the hard way that your default management style does not work with certain individuals or in certain situations. Moreover, you will become pigeon-holed into only knowing how to be successful in certain scenarios.

Effective implementation of the contingency approach means agility and flexibility so that you can be successful no matter what situation you face. Although there is merit to the old adage that there is no substitute for experience, using the contingency approach can help you learn faster from experiences, making fewer mistakes along the way.

Practice Golden-Rule 1 of Management in everything you do. Manage others the way you would like to be managed.
    —Brian Tracy

The STAR Manager vs. The DOPE Manager

The DOPE manager treats all of his employees the same. He maintains a rigid leadership style and forces a uniform decision-making style no matter the scenario.

The STAR manager adapts her decision-making and leadership style to best fit the situation and individuals involved, being mindful of both the situation's urgency and the stage of relationship she is in with her employees.

Explore Online: Management Basics Blueprint: On TheSparkSource.com, go to the Resources page to find a diagram and summary that details each of the basic attributes of the STAR manager. Then, find and take the STAR pre-assessment for the 10 Skills of STAR managers.

PART II
The 10 Skills of STAR Managers

The 10 skills discussed in the following chapters are attributes commonly developed by STAR managers. Each contributes to the exterior finish of the second-story addition to the house. In order to build and guide a consistently high-performing team, aspiring STAR managers must understand these traits and implement the best practices outlined here.

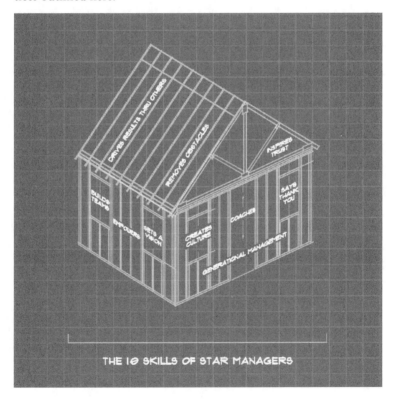

THE 10 SKILLS OF STAR MANAGERS

CHAPTER 8

Building an Unstoppable Team: Interviewing, Identifying Talent, and Hiring

What to Expect: Being a manager means many things, and among them is sitting on the opposite side of the interview table. This chapter discusses the end-to-end process of building a successful team, from screening and interviewing potential candidates to on-boarding new hires.

In most cases being a good boss means hiring talented people and then getting out of their way.

—Tina Fey

Too many companies believe people are interchangeable. Truly gifted people never are. They have unique talents. Such people cannot be forced into roles they are not suited for, nor should they be. Effective leaders allow great people to do the work they were born to do.

—Warren Bennis

Finally, a candidate who looked good! After screening dozens of resumes, I found a top performer with a great track record of results! I was looking forward to this interview. When we sat down in a conference room to talk, I had high hopes. After interviewing 16 other candidates I thought it would be "17th time's a charm."

As she started talking, not just a *word* but a *vivid mental image* came to mind: a bulldozer. She reminded me of a bulldozer.

This candidate had achieved great accolades in her past jobs and had concrete evidence proving this—she brought probably every framed certificate or trophy she ever received to the interview—but I knew that her great results came at a price. I did need a top performer but I could tell she would be a nightmare to manage. She probably would not be very responsive, nor would she have listened to a word I said (she could barely listen to the questions I asked her without talking over me). She was not a team player and would have thrown the team dynamic and culture I had created off balance. Despite how perfect she looked on paper, I decided to pass.

It took four more interviews, but finally, after interviewing more than 20 different candidates and looking at nearly 50 prescreened resumes, I found my ideal candidate. And it paid off. He was a great addition to the team, consistently delivering great results, and within a year was promoted because of his great work.

☆ ☆ ☆

I was recently at a tech conference and heard Richard Branson speak. He reminded me of an important truth: ***The most success-ful people surround themselves with people who are smarter than themselves and fill in their gaps.***

Such is the case for STAR managers.

In management roles, not only are you expected to manage the employees you are initially given, but you are also expected to hire new employees as others leave or the team expands. Your ability to identify and train exceptional people will separate you from the many DOPE managers in the working world.

You will be judged according to the people you hire and how they perform, even after you move on to a new position. This is not only a factor affecting team performance but also a factor affecting your reputation.

> **Quick Tip:** Does having a current job matter? Note whether the candidate you are interviewing currently has a job. Although this isn't always the case, the best candidates generally have their choice of where to go when they decide to leave their current job, and they ensure to secure a new job before leaving. Someone without a job could have been laid off for a legitimate reason outside of his control, or it may be a sign that he has issues that make him a less desirable candidate.

Effective hiring involves three distinct steps:

1. Screening and identifying solid candidates.
2. Interviewing and selecting the best candidates.
3. Integrating new hires into your team.

In keeping with the ever-famous "garbage in, garbage out" methodology, if you do not develop the ability to identify solid candidates, then the candidates you interview will be subpar, and your ability to integrate them into the team will not matter. The subsequent poor results from subpar people will put you at a disadvantage.

In a previous management role, I inherited two individuals who consistently performed well below expectations. I was in the process of taking them through a performance improvement plan that would likely lead to firing them when a peer of mine, who had recently been promoted, approached me about them. She was building a new team and both of my people had applied for the positions she had available. I was upfront about their poor performance and lack of improvement despite coaching.

Instead of heeding my advice, she decided to hire them under the rationale that they would pick up the job faster than an external hire because they already worked at the company. Throughout the next year, her team struggled to keep up with their job responsibilities, and after much effort she was able to fire one and convince the other to take a job better suited for his skills. Eventually, the team was dissolved and she was demoted back to a non-management role. If she had been more selective when choosing her people, she might still be a manager today. *When hiring, choose wisely.*

Screening and Identifying Solid Candidates

It's natural to feel overwhelmed when facing the task of hiring a new employee, but the key is to take one step at a time. The first step is to uncover a pool of potential candidates. The STAR manager knows that she must use her resources to find a large number of good candidates, so that there is a larger group from which to select the best.

As a rule, remember that a *human* connection is generally better than an *Internet* connection. The plethora of online job sites are fantastic resources, but when you have a personal connection to a candidate, it is much easier to discern whether he or she is the right fit. Generally a peer, direct report, or colleague can recommend someone they feel would be a good fit for the position.

Word of warning: Just because someone recommends a candidate does not mean that he or she is a good hire. As an aspiring STAR manager, you know the importance of the reputation you are building and that you have to stand behind any recommendations you make, but not everyone thinks that way.

There have been times when one of my direct reports has recommended a friend for a job opening. Although hiring this candidate may have been great for the morale of the one employee, I have found on numerous occasions that these candidates were far from the superstars I would want to hire. It is important to probe any person from whom you receive references to uncover how much they stand behind the person they are recommending. For my direct reports who have recommended someone, I make them commit to training the new hire and assuming responsibility for her work if the new hire does not meet expectation. This helps me quickly understand whether they believe in this candidate.

There is also the decision of whether to hire internally or externally. The transition will generally be faster and smoother if you search for someone who is already a company employee to fill your vacancy. Internal hires already understand your culture and business, internal acronyms used, and many of the systems you interact with. On the flip side, they may have developed some very bad habits or even complacency, and may lack the fresh perspective a candidate could bring if coming in from the outside. Don't let the short-term desire of quickly getting someone to produce results get in the way of finding the right person. An internal hire will produce results faster, but the results they produce may not be good.

It is important to cast a wide net. Besides asking your employees, your peers, your boss, and your networking connections, take a look at the other sources available. Search for people through industry networking groups, and use online portals like Monster, Glassdoor, CareerBuilder, and LinkedIn. Investigate your competitors and see if you can find a high-performing employee looking for something new. Be aware that your company will most likely have recruiting resources to help you find good candidates as well. Speak with your recruiters directly about the kind of candidate you are looking for so that they can tailor their search.

Once you have a set of resumes, it is important to screen them properly. Here are some key items to look for:

☆ **Past experience.** Ideally you are looking for someone who has already been successful at doing the job for which you are hiring. If not, look at what other experiences they do have that are relevant to what you are hiring for.

☆ **Numbers and impact.** Finding someone with matching past experience is great, but the results they achieved are much more important than just having experience. Don't act like a DOPE manager and be satisfied that they have experience. The STAR manager looks for someone with experience who was also able to drive results.

☆ **Amount of time at each company.** A diverse set of experiences may be good for building the foundation for a successful career, but jumping around between companies is concerning. Although unquestioned loyalty is a thing of the past, a complete lack of loyalty is bad. If a candidate has skipped from company to company in the past, he will continue to do so in the future. This means that you will spend time and effort training, only to have him leave before he actually starts contributing back to the team.

☆ **Lies or concerns on the resume.** You don't want someone who lacks integrity, so keep an eye out for anything misleading on a candidate's resume. One candidate I interviewed said he was getting his MBA at the UC Berkeley Extension School. Being an alumnus of UC Berkeley's Haas School of Business, I knew that the Extension School did not offer an MBA, just a certificate. When I pressed him about it in the interview, he lied to my face, saying he was getting his MBA. Don't be like him, or the short-lived Yahoo CEO Scott Thompson who lied on his resume and had his reputation forever tarnished.

Remember to be patient. There is no rush when finding the right people for your team. DOPEs fall into the "time trap." In sales, I was responsible for a quota, and even with six people on my team I had to ensure we sold seven people's worth of quota. In these situations (especially when your paycheck is affected), it is difficult to overlook the short-term pain to get long-term gain. STAR managers would rather take some months to find a 100-percent performer than hire a 60-percent performer immediately, who would ultimately take months (and endless amounts of effort) to fire.

This is why you should always "build a bench": identify and stay in contact with people you would want to hire for your team. Although you may not have an opening now, this funnel of top performers will help you fill future vacancies faster.

Now, after you have identified a number of good potential candidates, it's time to interview them.

> **Quick Tip:** A bonus of interviewing: The best way to become more effective when being interviewed is to gain experience as an interviewer. In the process of interviewing candidates, you see the types of things to do and not to do, which will be useful to keep in mind the next time you are interviewed.

Interviewing and Selecting the Best Candidates

The interview is the most important step in the process of building an unstoppable team. Experience will help you master reading people and testing whether someone is the right person for the job. It may seem uncomfortable at first, because most of us are used to *being* interviewed. As time goes on, however, you will become more comfortable with being on the other side of the interviewing table.

Here are some things to look for when interviewing someone:

☆ **The "DOPE to STAR" spectrum.** Seek out candidates who are STARs in a number of the 25 attributes outlined in Book One of the series (*The Young Professional's Guide to the Working World*) and who are DOPEs in few to none.

☆ **Leaders.** You want someone who knows how to adapt to fit her new role and will be a leader no matter what the situation.

☆ **Cultural fit.** As we will discuss in a later chapter, team culture is an important catalyst for consistent results. You don't want to add someone to the mix who will jeopardize your team dynamic.

☆ **Ease of transition and ramp-up.** You want someone who is a fast learner and is coachable, so that they catch on to their new job responsibilities and work environment quickly.

☆ **Initiative.** Employees who are self-guided and self-motivated are much better to manage and will go above and beyond when they take initiative.

☆ **Follow-through and overcoming adversity.** Every work environment will present its own challenges, and it is important to find people who will see a project through to its completion.

While physically conducting the interview, STAR managers set the right tone, ask the right questions, and probe and observe to uncover whether they have found the right candidate for the job. Here's how.

Set the Tone

The tone you set in the interview should fit your management style. Show your candidate the kind of manager you will be. Additionally, ensure that you take the following into consideration: Remember that in the interview, determining if a candidate is right for the position is not your only job. It is also your responsibility to sell her on the job, the company, and you as a manager. You are the most important success factor for her career, and if you indicate that you aren't there to help, solid candidates will not take the job.

☆ Don't power-trip. Resist the urge to show off or exert your authority when interviewing a candidate.

☆ Avoid informality. Watch out for candidates who immediately attempt to be your friend, or encourage you to be informal. The way she acts in the interview will only intensify if she gets the job. Moreover, you want to show her that despite your age, you mean business and are focused on running a high-performing team.

Ask the Right Questions

You will only be able to determine if you have a good candidate by asking the right questions. As a rule, it is better to ask behavioral questions that focus on past experience instead of hypothetical situations. Don't ask a candidate what she would do *if* she was in a certain situation; ask her to describe a past experience when she *was* in a situation similar to one she would face in the job she is interviewing for. It's easy for a candidate to give you an answer that would lead you to believe she fully understands the job if you ask a hypothetical, but if you ask for real-life examples, you can tell whether she has the relevant skills.

Be creative with the questions you ask and see how she thinks on her feet. The questions you ask will get at how much she understands your business, how interested she is in the position, and how much hard work she will put in to the job.

Here are some effective questions to ask during the interview:

☆ *Tell me about yourself/Take me through your resume.* This is the first shot at hearing her highlights as a candidate. It also shows whether the candidate can communicate concisely.

☆ *What are your strengths and weaknesses?* Be wary of cop-out responses to the weakness part, such as, "I take on too much," or, "I work too hard." Instead look for real weaknesses that the candidate started working to improve upon.

☆ *Tell me about a time when you faced a challenge.* All jobs involve dealing with challenges. You want to make sure the candidate can handle adversity.

☆ *Talk about a time you had to handle change.* Change is inevitable and you need people who can adapt.

☆ *Ask for quantifiable results.* In each reference to a job or experience, ensure that you have her specifically address her results, not just in general but also compared to her peers. In sales, for example, a candidate may be at 210-percent quota, which sounds good, but all her peers may be at 500 percent.

☆ *Past ratings.* Ask about previous performance reviews and the ratings she received.

☆ *What would your boss/coworkers say about you?* This is a great question to test a candidate's reputation.

☆ *Job-by-job analysis.* As a candidate talks about her experience, make it a point to specifically ask about the unique (hopefully positive) impact she left in her past jobs. It is also good to understand why she left a job. Was she fired? Did she consistently have conflicts with past bosses and coworkers? Generally a candidate will spin even being fired for the positive, but you will be able to see a track record of conflict, impatience, or entitlement.

☆ *Is there anything else you need to tell me?* This gives her the opportunity to take ownership of the interview and ensure she communicates things she planned to share with you. A great candidate will take this opportunity to share relevant experiences or traits she didn't address earlier in the interview.

☆ *Why should I hire you?* This is my favorite question to ask at the end of an interview. It allows you to see how well the candidate sells herself.

At the end of each interview, give the candidate an opportunity to ask questions. Pay close attention to the questions asked, because they are key indicators of how interested she is in the job and how much research she has done to prepare for the interview. Lame questions mean she is not very motivated or passionate about the job. Another key factor is whether she asks you what the next steps are in the interview process. Asking this shows she is interested in the position. I once had a peer who would not hire someone unless the candidate asked "What are the next steps?" at the end of the interview.

Probe and Observe

It is your responsibility to dig under the surface to accurately evaluate a candidate instead of just believing everything said. This involves probing to validate a candidate and being a good judge of character. A STAR manager is able to trust her gut when it indicates that something is not right about a candidate.

Once I was interviewing a candidate who looked great on paper. He was professional, seemed to have great experience, and talked as if he understood the job I was hiring for. My intuition was a bit uneasy, but I decided to stick to the facts. I hired him, and unfortunately found out soon after that he was only good on the surface. He ended up being a slow learner and a poor performer. I should have trusted my gut.

Because so many jobs today involve working with a team, it is important to validate the candidate's role and impact on the team and not just the team's results. We have all been on teams in which some people don't pull their weight but take credit for the results. You don't want this type of person on your team.

Part of the probing process should involve using your peers or boss to validate top candidates. They will be able to see things you don't and can be a big help in the process, especially when you have narrowed the field to a small number of quality candidates. A STAR manager also considers having candidates interview with her direct reports. She wants to confirm that any new hire will partner well with the rest of the team.

Finally, it is important to check references. Ensure that the past references a candidate provides are past bosses with positive feedback and not just their friends. It is also a good practice to validate accomplishments. In the process of hiring one employee, I asked for evidence of the awards he said he received, requesting he scan and e-mail me photocopies and photos of the certificates and awards.

☆ ☆ ☆

Now it's time to finalize your selection and share the decision with your candidates. When informing a candidate you did not choose about your decision, be direct and provide constructive criticism so she can improve. If you can share why you didn't select her, it may help her get another job.

Integrating New Hires into Your Team

Integrating a new hire starts the moment you inform her that she has the job. As part of the same conversation, it's important to start preparing her for success. Assign some tasks to help her become ready to hit the ground running. Offer training resources and things to sharpen up on.

Once she starts working, formally introduce her to the team. Talk up the new hire with her new peers and help her connect with people who can help her, while uncovering ways she can contribute to other members of the team. Your other employees will be more willing to help if they see a way they can benefit in the process.

Assign a formal mentor, generally someone you are grooming for promotion. Concurrently, schedule training sessions for your new hire with team members who are good at specific systems, tasks, or projects. They can be mini-mentors, teaching the new hire good habits and best practices from the beginning.

Throughout the process, it is important you monitor how your new hire is transitioning. Check in to see how she fits with the team culture. Validate that she is learning the right things from assigned trainings and keep an eye out for any early problems.

Hiring new employees can be one of the most challenging roles of a manager. STAR managers know that when they work hard to identify the right candidates through a variety of channels, effectively interview and select the best ones, and then properly integrate these new hires into the team, they will create an environment where new employees thrive.

Surround yourself with great people; delegate authority; get out of the way.

—Ronald Reagan

The STAR Manager vs. The DOPE Manager

The DOPE manager is more concerned with coming off as an authority figure during the interview process—showing his control. He rushes through the hiring process, more concerned with getting short-term results than patiently searching for and finding the candidate who will drive long-term results.

The STAR manager takes hiring very seriously and puts forth a great deal of effort to identify, analyze, and select the right employees. Once selected, she ensures candidates are on the road to success by executing a proactive on-boarding plan.

Explore Online: On TheSparkSource.com Resources page you will find the "STAR Manager's Interview Guide," which will assist you in evaluating job candidates and on-boarding new hires.

CHAPTER 9

Creating Focus: Building Your Team Vision and Goals

What to Expect: STAR managers set a clear path and end goal for their teams. This chapter explores why it is important to set a team vision, discusses the process to create team goals and a vision, and teaches how to avoid letting the team veer off course. The importance of creating a balance between getting input from your team and making the strategy uniquely your own is also discussed.

A leader is one who knows the way, goes the way, and shows the way.
—John C. Maxwell

"Would you tell me, please, which way I ought to go from here?"

"That depends a good deal on where you want to go to," said the cat.

"I don't care much where..." said Alice.

"Then it doesn't matter which way you go," said the cat.

—Lewis Carroll (*Alice in Wonderland*)

"The key to success this year is RIP," I proclaimed as I turned the portable whiteboard to unveil its front side to my team during a meeting a few years ago. Amidst some giggles and a couple eye rolls, I explained the meaning of the giant R-I-P written in large block letters on the board.

RIP was my acronym for the year, which outlined our keys to success. The acronym stood for the following: R for Relationships (networking relationships), I for IP (Internet protocol, a suite of products that was the most lucrative at helping reach our sales quotas), and P for Processes (the back-end processes and procedures that the team struggled with previously, which kept us from selling more). In a previous year, the acronym was FRIK and another year it was NOS (with an obvious connection to the boost it gives cars in drag racing—that year we needed to create some momentum). A bit corny? Yes. Memorable and simple? Absolutely. But most importantly, it worked. Through this strategy to create focus, my team was able to achieve the top results that year (and the other acronyms guided my teams to be #1 for three years in a row).

As a manager, one of your major roles is to guide your team to accomplishing ***goals***. The primary compass that will direct your goals (which in turn drives your results) is your ***vision***. A team's vision outlines the focus and dictates why you do what you do. STAR managers work with their teams to create both. ***A vision is a desired end state.*** Generally, it is a statement that encapsulates what the world would look like if the team attained all it wanted to accomplish. ***Goals***, on the other hand, ***are more focused and specific.***

(I will spare everyone the "SMART goals" breakdown. By this point, I am sure you have heard about it ad nauseam. For a refresher, look it up online.) Goals characterize something specific that the team wants to accomplish, such as improving report processing time by 50 percent or bringing a new product to market before a deadline. Goals are shorter-term and more defined than a vision.

The process and guidelines described in this chapter can be used in both vision- and goal-creation and attainment.

Why Creating Goals and a Vision Is Important

Most people are goal-driven to varying degrees, and without a defined desired end-state, or "point B," it is more challenging to determine whether you ever reach your destination. Your team's vision and, on a smaller scale, goals, create that "point B" for which everyone can aim.

Visions and goals make sure that everyone is headed in the right direction, together.

STAR managers are forward-thinking. As Brian Tracy puts in his book, *How The Best Leaders Lead*, effective leaders have foresight. They are strategic thinkers who develop an ability to anticipate trends and obstacles, constantly thinking about the future. Peter Drucker, whom many consider to be the father of modern management, illustrates this point when he asserts that one of a manager's roles is to manage objectives, in addition to workers and the business itself.

How to Craft a Team Vision and Goals

When creating your team's vision, it is important that it follows the SAR formula. The letters stand for **SIMPLE**, **ALIGNED**, and **REPEATED**.

First and foremost, the vision and goals must be **SIMPLE**. If a vision or set of goals is too complicated, no one will ever remember it, let alone understand what it really means. Acronyms can be very helpful in creating a team's focus, but, though you may be tempted to throw in a few extra letters or add in one additional core value, this will dilute the message. I remember seeing a team vision that was organized to spell out CUSTOMER. The word *customer* has eight letters. EIGHT. To this day I couldn't tell you what a single letter represented. Three to four letters is fine. That's why RIP, FRIK, and NOS were so effective for my teams.

If you choose to go with a statement in your vision, don't make it a five-part sentence. Make sure it is direct.

Goals tend to be more quantitative but should not be too de-tailed and complicated, otherwise it will lead to discouragement for your team. A solid goal is something like, "Decrease project turn-around time by 25 percent while maintaining an error rate of less than 10 percent." If it were written, "Decrease priority project turn-around time by 35 percent and standard project turnaround time by 25 percent while not generating any processing errors through the first three stages of submission and review while leveraging a 24-hour response time to any rejects or information queries," you lost everyone long before reaching the end of the sentence. Both goals and vision should be consumable and easy to explain to people both within and outside of your team.

Team goals and visions must also be **ALIGNED**, not only with each other but also among all the stakeholders the team serves, in-cluding the individual team members and your boss. When build-ing goals and a vision, make sure they are in sync with your boss's directives and focus. If your boss's main focus is expanding into new strategic areas, then your vision and goals should center on this. To ensure buy-in from your boss, be sure to get confirmation that the team's goals and vision are aligned.

Team goal/vision creation should involve collaboration between you and your team. Ultimately you will need to guide your team to ensure alignment with your boss and department leadership, but it is important to tap into your team's creativity to craft your goals and vision. This not only uncovers new and creative ideas, but also empowers your employees to take ownership of attaining the vision and goals because they were part of the process. A good starting point is to ask your team what they want to accomplish.

The ultimate determinant in the adoption of a team vision is the meaning your employees place behind achieving the team vision and striving to accomplish goals. When your team buys in, great things happen.

Despite the importance of getting input, make sure to leave your mark on the vision and goals created. You are still the boss and should find a way to make it your own. This will keep you engaged and motivate you to push your team toward success.

> **Quick Tip:** When creating a team vision and goals, be real. Don't choose some goal that you know is completely unattainable, as this demotivates the team. In the same vein, don't choose a generic goal like "have fun." This usually shows up as an afterthought, and many employees will not take it seriously.

The best way to characterize proper alignment is to realize that the team's *vision* must support your people, *goals* must support the team's vision, and *projects*, *tasks*, and *assignments* must support the team's goals.

Finally, the team's goals and vision must be **REPEATED**. Effective goal/vision attainment does not come just from spending time developing goals, but instead from taking action. STAR managers require accountability from their team to accomplish goals. The simplest way to keep goals and visions top-of-mind is to talk about them. For example, I would reference RIP during every team meeting and even during one-on-one coaching sessions with my employees. When we succeeded, I pointed out where the success to the R, I, or P categories was in our RIP mantra. When we fell short, I referenced which area needed to improve. Then, when a directive came down from my boss that required the team to change from business-as-usual, I related the change to how it supported our vision and goals. I brought my portable whiteboard to every single team meeting and would actually point to the applicable letter. Each year, I reviewed the team focus with my employees until they had all internalized it.

A manager's responsibility for formulating goals and visions does not stop at the team level. STAR managers also know that it is their job to help their employees establish and work toward their own individual goals. Empowering your team to dream big and work hard to accomplish their goals will help you achieve team goals—when you make an effort to ensure your team goals are aligned with the goals of each individual on your team.

Taking Action on the Team's Goals and Vision

As a manager, you must fill three distinct roles throughout the vision/goal development process.

1. **Visionary.** Often your employees won't be able to connect the dots between where the team currently is and where it should be as effectively as you can. It is your job to show the team the connections among their individual goals, the team's goals, and the desired end state. STAR managers paint a picture of why a certain vision is what the team should adopt, then motivate everyone to believe it can be achieved.

2. **Catalyst.** Effective managers foster action. They empower teams to move forward instead of standing still. STAR managers get people out of their comfort zone and give employees a reason to do their best.

3. **Task-master.** DOPE managers may be effective at putting together a cohesive vision and aligned goals but drop off in follow-through. Making goals is easy; achieving them is difficult. STAR managers foster self- and peer discipline and

make sure that at all times the team knows where they are in relation to achieving their goals.

When building a team vision and team goals, be bold and un-afraid. Take risks and push the team to focus on a goal farther than they initially think is attainable. At the same time, ensure that you get input from your team and that you are aligned with your boss. Realize that the path to your team's vision and goals won't be direct, and know that you have to be the main driver to ensure everyone reaches the finish line.

> *Great leaders are almost always great simplifiers, who can cut through argument, debate, and doubt to offer a solution everybody can understand.*
> —Gen. Colin Powell

> *Direction, not intention, determines destination.*
> —Andy Stanley

The STAR Manager vs. The DOPE Manager

The DOPE Manager gets caught up in developing a simple and aligned vision and goals but is often unable to follow through in attaining milestones set.

The STAR Manager masters developing goals and a team vision and goes one step further by focusing her team on accomplishing them through continual reference and accountability.

CHAPTER 10

Your Team Is Like a Family: Getting Buy-In, Support, and Trust

What to Expect: Sometimes managing a team can mimic running a family. Building strong relationships within your team makes the difference between good teams and great teams. STAR managers gain employee buy-in, garner support for both themselves and their employees, and create a trusting environment. This chapter discusses how to gain buy-in and how to foster trust within your team.

Always recognize that human individuals are ends, and do not use them as means to your end.

—Immanuel Kant

117

You can't grow long-term if you can't eat short-term.
Anybody can manage short. Anybody can manage long. Bal-
ancing those two things is what management is.

—Jack Welch

Imagine a team has all the right ingredients for success: talented team members, abundant resources, strong management, a solid plan, and a track record of individual successes. In many cases, this recipe leads to outstanding results; however, with even one ingredient missing, success is not probable. That one ingredient is *teaming*, acting as a single unit and not as a compilation of individuals.

Such was the case for the 2004 U.S. Olympic basketball team. This team had superstars like LeBron James and Tim Duncan, and a coach in Larry Brown who had brought teams to win both NBA and NCAA National Championships. Yet they had only five wins and three losses, barely eking out a bronze medal and winning games by an average of 4.6 points (compared to the 44-point victory margin of the 1992 Dream Team). Although there are many diagnoses for why a team that had so much more talent and resources than any other team in the world did not win, the true cause is clear: they didn't play like a team. They didn't fully create the main building blocks that every team needs to work as a cohesive unit: trust, positive working relationships, and buy-in.

Talent, resources, and a well-thought-out plan are not enough. As a manager, you have more influence than anyone else on the degree of trust, strong relationships, and buy-in present among your team. In fact, the way successful managers create high-performing teams is by making sure their employees truly act as a team.

The important thing the DOPE manager forgets and the STAR manager always has in the forefront of her mind is that **employees are people, not just results.** If you manage just the results rather than people, you will not be able to create the environment needed to succeed.

The best way to keep your focus on the *person* rather than the *result* is to not assume control or power over someone. Doing so can lead you to violate his trust and force him to do things without his buy-in, ultimately damaging your working relationship. The STAR manager realizes that she must continuously maintain this trust and buy-in after developing it. Although an occasional slip-up may happen, a blatant violation will keep her from maximizing her employees' performance.

As referenced, there are three primary factors needed to create a consistently high-performing team unit in which people remain more important than results. These ways create:

1. Trust among the team.

2. Strong working relationships.

3. Buy-in for team goals and processes.

Trust and Ethics

As Stephen M.R. Covey asserts in his book *The Speed of Trust*, *trust* means to have confidence in the integrity and the abilities of another.

Trust must be established first. Trust lays a foundation made of the knowledge that you will follow through with what you commit to. It also communicates to your team that you believe in them and that you will have your employees' backs when challenges arise. With a team, there is an exponential effect such that its sum is greater than its individual members.

The importance of trust is clearly seen in how situations play out when there is a lack of trust. Without trust, everyone works for themselves and assumes other team members have ulterior motives. People don't help each other. There is often a lack of communication, so ideas are guarded and warnings are not passed along. People may support each other in public, but behind closed doors contention surfaces.

In Stephen R. Covey's (Stephen M.R. Covey's father) book *Principle-Centered Leadership*, he talks of the perils of low trust. Cynicism becomes the default, the individual comes ahead of the team, and accusations begin to abound.

The following are a number of ways to create a sense of trust. Most are simple and straightforward, but they must be kept in mind; trust can get lost amidst day-to-day responsibilities if left unmonitored.

- ☆ **Trust yourself.** Team trust starts with the trust you put in your own abilities as a manager. We serve as role models for our teams. The character and competence we show (as explained by Stephen M.R. Covey) will either foster trust and a sense of team or will create factions and skepticism. Your employees will not trust you if you don't trust them.

- ☆ **See things from their point of view.** It is often tough to take a step back and look at the basics when you get busy and responsibility kicks in. To build trust, you must to make an effort to see where your employees are coming from instead of just thinking about what you want to accomplish.

- ☆ **Follow through.** In *The Leadership Challenge*, Jim Kouzes and Barry Posner keenly point out that **credibility is the foundation of leadership.** The way to create this credibility, and ultimately trust, from your team comes when you see your commitments through to completion. Be careful what you promise your team and ensure that you follow through on what you promise.

- ☆ **Explain the *why* to the team.** Trust develops when everyone is on the same page. If you do not explain *why* you make certain decisions, *why* the team needs to achieve a certain goal, or *why* to follow a directive, your employees may comply in the short term, but you may lose their trust and focus in the long run. If you are not comfortable with a certain reason *why* you are asking your team to do something, consider whether the request may be based in bad intent or may be in your selfish best interests over the team's.

☆ **Be consistent.** Consistency gives your employees an indication of how you will act in a certain situation. If you reward good actions and discipline behavior that violates the trust of the team or are selfish in nature, then the team will tend to avoid negative actions and will seek ways to be rewarded.

☆ **Be transparent.** Don't hide your true intentions or keep things that are important to your team behind closed doors. If you make secrecy a normal practice, your team will consider that you have ulterior motives and will not trust you. When you are more transparent, your team will not only trust you but will also help with the things you share with them. *Note*: there are times when you cannot share certain things with your team; for example, if your boss makes you aware of a possible organization restructuring before a formal announcement, it may be best to wait before freaking your team out by telling them.

☆ **Admit when you don't know.** DOPE leaders feel that they must be the rock for their team and that they must know the answer to every question and know what to do in any situation. The STAR manager admits when she doesn't know something and actively asks her employees for help. By doing this, her team trusts and respects her more.

☆ **Unity.** As referenced with the 2004 Olympic U.S. basketball team, a strong team that trusts each other is not solely a smattering of individuals; it is a single unit. Teams that trust each other stand behind each other and work as one for the goals of the team. Treating the group as a team that must rely on each other, instead of just a set of individuals, builds trust.

Once this trust is created, a number of benefits follow, including:

☆ **Open communication.** The presence of trust creates an environment where people can speak their minds and help both your employees, and you as a manager, improve.

☆ **The foundation for comfort and momentum.** For a team to reach consistent high performance, trust is needed. With trust present, a positive momentum flourishes, making results improve exponentially.

☆ **Follow-through on commitments.** When trust exists and you set a good example, your people will be more committed to following through with their commitments. This allows you to have confidence that when you delegate a task or set a deadline, your team will ensure they meet your standards.

☆ **Mutual respect.** The presence of trust fosters a sense of respect among the team, and ultimately people will treat each other the way they want to be treated.

Quick Tip: It's okay if your employees don't invite you to lunch. Remember that you don't need to be their friend to effectively manage them. You have enough of your own friends outside of work, and you were not promoted to manager for the purpose of making more friends.

Strong Working Relationships

Part of being mindful that your employees are people and not just results is building a relationship with them. A positive relationship must be present to foster trust.

Building a solid working relationship with your employees can happen in many ways. I once hired an employee who moved halfway across the country to be on my team. He had to uproot his life and move to a new city where he didn't know anyone. Shortly after moving, he mentioned to me that he needed to see a dentist. I recommended my dentist and helped him get in touch to set up an appointment. He ended up needing dental surgery and wouldn't be able to drive home from the dentist's office. Knowing that he didn't have anyone to give him a ride, I offered to take him home, stopping by the pharmacy along the way to pick up his medication.

This didn't take much time for me, but it meant a great deal to my new employee. He could see that I really cared about him, not only as an employee who was driving results, but also as a person. My sensitivity toward his "out of his comfort zone" situation of moving to a new city led me to find other ways to help him get settled, creating a great working relationship in the process.

One of the best ways to build a relationship with your employees is to learn what is important to them and make sure to talk about it with them. For some employees it may be their kids or other family members. For others it may be travel. The genuine interest I take in something important to them helps develop our working relationship and shows that I care for them as people.

At the core of relationship-building is empathy. As Bob Wall expresses in his book *Working Relationships*, this is a foundational ingredient for building relationships that takes discipline and centering on other people. Empathy is key in understanding your employees' perspectives when making decisions and pushing them to perform at the highest level.

The relationships you build with your team (and that they build with each other) are multifaceted. A strong working relationship has both a professional and a personal side to it. When you balance both, people are more willing to work hard for you.

Simultaneously, don't let personal and professional relationships blend together too much. If you are a friend of one of your employees outside of work, it is important not to let that friendship affect your managerial decisions. Showing them favoritism or purposely giving them worse treatment is a recipe for disaster.

Buy-In

Buy-in from your team is a key element in creating a sense of team unity as well as trust in you as a leader. Buy-in is the commitment and follow-through from your team stemming from the belief that you are leading them down the right path. The vision you create with your team will not be successful without buy-in from each and every one of your direct reports.

Once you have established strong working relationships and trust among your employees, here are the ways to capture their buy-in:

☆ **Ask your employees for ideas ahead of time and feedback afterward.** If you ask for your team's ideas, they will not only feel valued but will also be more committed to the direction you set. By including your employees in the process, you will be exposed to ideas that you may not have thought of. Numerous times my team's ideas (not mine) have developed into very successful strategies because it's easier for people to buy in when it was originally their idea.

☆ **Explain the WIIFM (What's In It For Me).** Letting your team know what's in it for them will help them connect the direction you set and decisions you make with the benefits that will come to the team and each of them as individuals.

☆ **Support something important to your team.** Just as in networking, STAR managers seek to help others first. By supporting something important to your employees, they will be more motivated to buy in to working on initiatives that are important to you. Something as simple as challenging an administrative policy change that your team is against will pay dividends.

☆ **Have humility.** A recent *San Francisco Chronicle* article ("Taking a Cue from Bochy") analyzed multiple-World-Series-winning coach of the San Francisco Giants, Bruce Bochy. In writing the article, Kathleen Pender asked a number of business leaders and management thinkers what makes Bochy successful as a baseball coach. A common response was Bochy's humility. Quoting an article by Jim Collins, Pender illustrates that Bochy is a "Level 5 Leader" because he "demonstrates compelling modesty, shuns public adulation and is never boastful." By acting in this manner, your people will rally behind your leadership and buy in to your vision because they see that your primary interest is team success rather than personal gain.

☆ **Build consensus.** Consensus-building takes the concept of asking for advice from your team and making them a part of the decision-making process to a new level. Although you will not be able to get full agreement on every decision from everyone (nor would I recommend trying), for important priorities and goals, your team will buy in if you not only ask their opinion, but also get them to agree to the path forward ahead of time.

Establishing buy-in will provide you with the ability to enact your initiatives. Buy-in particularly becomes valuable when you need short spurts of intense effort from the team. To get people out of their comfort zones and work them harder than even they think they can work, you need to have their buy-in. This buy-in, paired with motivation and empowerment, is an invaluable resource that STAR managers develop.

The Power of "We"

The final tool that STAR managers use to build trust, develop strong working relationships, and get buy-in is leveraging the power of "we."

Most managers were top performers as individual contributors. So, as a top performer, you are used to the spotlight. But as a manager, you must have the team's interests in mind. Building a sense of team means creating the concept of "we" among the group.

In the *Harvard Management Update* article "Moving From Me To We," Anne Field explains that if you focus on your own performance (or think in terms of "me"), then your people may go over your head to your boss. She states that seeing how you are perceived by your direct reports is a common measurement for how effective you are at creating a team feel. Your employees will not align with your goals if they see them as only serving you and not the team (or themselves).

A sense of "we" fosters collaboration within your team and generates a trusting environment where your employees can comfortably innovate and contribute.

☆ ☆ ☆

Talent and a great plan can lead to some success. But for consistent top results, creating a true sense of a team among your employees is essential. Leverage trust, your working relationships, and your buy-in to continuously succeed no matter the obstacles the team faces. Even without team members whose talents parallel those of an Olympic basketball team, you will be able to help your team achieve amazing results that far surpass the sum of what each individual could accomplish.

> *Start with the end in mind.*
> —Stephen R. Covey

The STAR Manager vs. The DOPE Manager

The DOPE manager skips ahead to directing his team instead of learning about them as individuals and making sure trust and support exists. He is more likely to follow a "because I said so" methodology instead of getting genuine buy-in.

The STAR manager knows that she must first built trust within her team (both in her as a manager and among her employees) before getting the team to perform at its potential. She builds strong working relationships and gets buy-in before moving forward with initiatives.

CHAPTER 11

Constructing Your Team's Culture: The Environment You Create Sets the Tone

What to Expect: In the same way your communication affects what your employees focus on, the culture you create will have a tremendous effect on how they interact with each other, how they treat you, and what behaviors they adopt. This chapter talks about the benefits of trusting and supportive cultures and how to create the ideal culture for the team's vision.

Good management is the art of making problems so interesting and their solutions so constructive that everyone wants to get to work and deal with them.

—Paul Hawken

I think that the best training a top manager can be engaged in is management by example.

—Carlos Ghosn

"Team, we are having a great month so far. We are ahead of targets and it looks like there are a number of good opportunities in our funnels that are going to close. Awesome job! Let's keep it up!" I exclaimed.

All of a sudden I heard shots go off. *Click, click. BOOM!* Two shotgun blasts sounded. Shocked, my eyes darted all over the room. As I scanned the conference table, I realized that two of my employees were cocking and firing their shotgun iPhone apps in celebration of our great results.

"Geez, guys!" I groaned, as the entire team burst into laughter.

It wasn't quite my idea of how to celebrate a team win, but it fit the style of my direct reports, so I went with it. I then commended one of my other employees for helping train the team on a new system, and, upon finishing, pointed to the two "iPhone gunmen" in the room. They fired off another round amidst laughter from the team.

Just as a culture defines a group of people from a specific country or ethnic background, so does it define a team. The culture that you create within your team is an important factor that contributes to your success as a manager. As shown in my conference-room situation, team culture develops from a combination of the work atmosphere you want to create and the people who make up your team. Your team's culture is a mixture of the norms, processes, and working environment your team operates in, as well as the way people interact with each other and with you.

Culture is so important for a team, because it sets the tone for the group and motivates your employees to either work hard and stay focused, or become distracted and pursue selfish goals. The culture you allow to develop will either make your employees (and you) want to come into the office each day because they enjoy their job or will lead them to dread being a part of your team.

What Great Team Cultures Are Made Of

You should strive to create your own unique team culture by effectively using the contingency approach (detailed in Chapter 7), but there are a number of elements present in any high-performing team's culture. Here are the ingredients STAR managers choose from to craft their recipe for an optimal team culture.

☆ **A true *team*.** This may seem obvious, but STAR managers don't want a group of individuals, instead opting for a team that operates as a single unit. A team of superstars may be great in theory, but in practice it can create a toxic culture.

☆ **Trust and buy-in.** As mentioned in Chapter 10, trust and buy-in are core elements that must be present before you can create the team culture that will help your team thrive.

☆ **Goal alignment.** When your employees' goals are aligned with team goals and everyone's actions are focused on achieving these goals, you will have a strong team culture.

☆ **Empowered STAR employees.** Managers want proactive people with STAR qualities. This, paired with empowerment, generates an environment where people will accomplish great things.

☆ **A mix of informality and formality.** Healthy team cultures have a mix of formality and informality. Professionalism (a key form of formality) and the goals of the team should be present, but informality creates the glue that holds the team together in tough times.

☆ **Positive mindset.** Negativity is not allowed in the atmosphere of optimal team cultures. DOPE managers let negativity permeate, while STAR managers insist that the team think positively and reframe issues as opportunities and challenges to be tackled.

☆ **Belief in you as a leader.** You want a team culture in which your employees believe in and listen to you. Just as belief is a key ingredient to motivating and empowering employees, it is also a key factor in getting your team to accept the culture you create.

☆ **Honesty.** Honesty and integrity are imperatives for a successful team culture. Not only must honesty be present in your employees' work, but there must be honesty in both the feedback you give your team and the feedback they give you.

☆ **Helping attitude.** STAR managers want their employees to help each other. Whether that manifests itself formally through peer coaching or more informally on an ad hoc basis, successful teams have a culture of helping each other.

☆ **Supportiveness.** Healthy team cultures are supportive. STAR managers create a sense of perspective in failure and an environment where people support each other when they are struggling, motivating each other to improve.

☆ **Communication and collaboration.** Effective team cultures must have open communication and collaboration. It is okay if people openly disagree and identify problems as long as they work together to find solutions. High-performing teams are made of people who don't take things personally.

☆ **Learning and development.** High-performing teams are constantly learning and developing. By creating a culture in which learning and developing is valued (including having time specifically set aside to develop people), your employees will be more engaged and committed to achieving the goals you set.

☆ **Flexibility and agility.** Things will go wrong, and with constant change, old methods will need to be rethought. At one point, during a particularly hard year, I bought a chameleon Beany Baby that I used as a metaphor for the team, reminding them that we have to be flexible and constantly change to reach our goals the way chameleons colors change to survive.

☆ **Accountability and ownership.** Toxic team environments are characterized by finger pointing as everyone blames each other for failures. STAR managers develop a sense of accountability and ownership among the team for the work that each team member produces. This ingredient creates a self-checking process so the team monitors itself, along with a sense of pride in the work your team does.

☆ **Resiliency.** Teams will fail. A healthy team culture is one of resiliency, as people pick each other up when they fall and overcome obstacles because the group knows they are just part of the pathway to success.

☆ **Rewards and recognition.** When you create a culture in which people are rewarded and recognized for accomplishing their goals, your employees will work harder because of the recognition they get.

☆ **Consistency.** Effective team cultures are consistent. DOPE managers create a culture that may make people feel fulfilled amidst success, but not when the team fails. STAR managers uphold a consistent culture regardless of external factors.

☆ **Fun.** This may sound like a cliché, but fun is a key ingredient of a healthy team culture. It is important to both create fun and allow your team to find their own fun. For example, when sharing industry news with my team during our weekly meetings, I once referred to the online game Second Life where people create an avatar and live in a digital world. After mentioning this, my team made a comment (at least once during each team meeting for the next year) that poked fun at how I spent every night at home playing Second Life by myself (even though I never really had played the game). Remember that it's okay when the right culture is created at your expense.

☆ **Sense of impact.** Many tout the great cultures of companies like Google where employees get free meals and on-site massages or dentists, but no matter how "cool" a group's culture is, it becomes old, boring, and demotivating in time when the employees perceive they aren't learning or making a real impact. Ensure that the team culture is focused on having an impact.

☆ **Results focus.** In the book *Execution: The Discipline of Getting Things Done*, Larry Bossidy, Ram Charan, and Charles Burck say that execution, which leads to achievement, must be a core element of a team's culture that is integrated into recognition programs and behavioral norms. Without maintaining a clear focus on results, actions and processes will lead the team further away from its goals.

> **Quick Tip:** Help your people, don't command them. Remember that your people still have the free will to choose to obey you or not. If you command them instead of creating a healthy environment, they may seem as though they are aligned with you face-to-face, but will not support you when your back is turned.

How to Create the Right Team Culture

Now that we have outlined the elements that make up a healthy team culture, let's focus on the methods you can use to create the optimal team culture. This process can be difficult, especially when resistance exists.

I once managed a team with one top performer who had a very strong will and a dominant personality. Through a reorg, I received a team of new people (including this top performer) and had to adapt the current team culture to better fit my management style. A power struggle ensued. The top performer was used to doing whatever he wanted and calling the shots with old managers. He fought back, but I held strong to my principles and insisted that every team member follow a set of clear rules. After putting him on a coaching plan because of his poor leadership, he finally gave in and became a supporter of the team culture I wanted for the team.

The following are 10 key ways to develop the culture you feel is best for your team.

1. **Get everyone on the same page.** STAR managers ensure that everyone on their team understands team goals, values, and processes, and buys in to them. People who share the same culture have aligned values. STAR managers paint a picture of a common worldview.

2. **Be among the people.** DOPE managers separate themselves from their teams, seeing themselves as above their employees. STAR managers know that in order to understand and connect with their teams, they must be among them.

3. **Ensure everyone is engaged.** Just as engagement is a prerequisite for empowerment, it is also needed for effectively developing your team's culture. People need to be engaged to adopt your culture; otherwise, they will rebel and stay within their comfort zones.

4. **Connect the team personally.** STAR managers implement the appropriate team culture by connecting to their employees and ensuring that they connect to each other. In the book *Working Relationships*, author Bob Wall explains that it's much easier to work with people with whom you feel connected on a personal level.

5. **Create consensus and allow dissent.** To effectively adopt a new culture, a manager must get each team member to agree upon the best culture to create. Don't squash dissent. Dissenters are valuable because they not only help strengthen the culture you want to create by poking holes in it, but they can also provide a new perspective that you may want to integrate into your team culture.

6. **Connect the desired culture to team results.** STAR managers connect the desired culture to achieving both team and personal goals so that employees believe that adopting this culture will make them more successful.

7. **Be a good example.** You must serve as an example for the culture you want to create. If you want to create a culture of collaboration, ensure that you solicit opinions and create groups when assigning projects. Make sure the culture not only fits the situation and employees, but also your management style.

8. **Facilitate the culture you want to create.** Your management and monitoring of team culture adoption means the difference between a cohesive and aligned team environment and one that is out of control. Focus on objectives and not problems, reward when your team upholds your desired culture, and discipline when the team does not.

9. **Reflect.** STAR managers reflect on their team culture, taking a step back in the face of daily pressures to get a clearer look. Change environments to encourage reflection by planning a team outing or offsite meeting. This not only helps in the reflection process, but also facilitates supportiveness and collaboration.

10. **Be willing to adapt.** An effective team culture is not static. It is an ever-changing team force. STAR managers are willing to adapt their team cultures as situations change.

Once you develop and implement the optimal culture for your team, you will see an increase in employee engagement, empowerment to proactively take action, heightened momentum in achieving goals, and an overall higher morale.

Because a team culture must be constantly adapted, open lines of communication and two-way feedback must be utilized to keep a pulse on the team. Clear reminders and norms that facilitate this agility are important for high-performing teams.

Cleaning up a Toxic Team Culture

You will find that there will be times when people won't get along, trust will be challenged, and people will act selfishly. Whereas each unique situation merits a different response, a STAR manager knows that she must always be the steward for the culture she desires to create. She stops the development of a toxic culture by making team culture a topic of conversation. When situations challenge the team culture, she brings them up with the team. When certain individuals are not adopting the right culture or attitude, she speaks with them individually and establishes clear consequences for a lack of compliance. Although there are times when she must use a heavy hand, she ensures that her employees know it is for the betterment of the team and that she has the success of each individual in mind when crafting and normalizing the team's culture.

A team culture manifests itself in many different ways, from team traditions to accepted rules and even norms for interacting. No matter what the makeup of your team's culture, it is an important factor that determines the level of success your team achieves. More importantly, it is the factor you have the most influence on, and you must work hard to establish and maintain it.

> *All organizations are perfectly designed to get the results they are now getting. If we want different results, we must change the way we do things.*
> —Tom Northup

The STAR Manager vs. The DOPE Manager

The DOPE manager lets the individuals on his team or the pressures of the job dictate the type of work environment his team exists in. He selfishly pursues what is in his best interests and makes the team follow him, leading them to be less engaged and unfocused.

The STAR manager understands the importance of an optimal team culture. She works hard to develop a sense of team and shows her team how their goals align with those of the team. She serves as an example for the culture she wants to create and instills in her team a sense that they are making an impact.

CHAPTER 12

Managers Are Coaches: Developing Your Team Through Feedback and Beyond

What to Expect: A manager's central responsibility is to develop the individuals on her team, and one of her most important roles is as a coach. STAR managers leverage feedback and coaching techniques to help individuals on their team reach peak performance. This chapter explores coaching and feedback techniques that not only improve team performance but also identify areas of improvement for you as a manager.

> *The conventional definition of management is getting work done through people, but real management is developing people through work.*
> —Agha Hasan Abedi

What's measured improves.

—Peter F. Drucker

It is easy to miss out on the basics, especially in the fast-paced business world.

Even today, famous UCLA basketball coach John Wooden's philosophy still rings true. He took his teams back to the fundamentals. Instead of starting with the details of passing and shooting, he started at the very beginning. He taught his players how to properly put on their socks and tie their shoes. His reasoning: wearing socks correctly prevents blisters and properly tied shoes reduce the risk of ankle injury risk. No matter how many cool dunks you can make with healthy feet, it is painful or impossible with blisters or a sprained ankle. Besides being loved by his former players and generations of fans, his unmatched record of 10 national championships validates his philosophy.

STAR managers know that they are coaches for their team. It is rare to be assigned a team of top performers that require no guidance. STAR managers work hard to build their teams to reach their potential. Sometimes this occurs through big breakthroughs and other times it involves reminding an employee of the fundamentals, or offering an outside perspective.

As Sheila Murray Bethel points out in her book *Making a Difference*, a leader is a team builder who maximizes people's potential. Bethel asserts that in team-building there are two cardinal rules: (1) Praise in public and correct in private, and (2) praise what is right and train to change what is wrong.

These rules encapsulate the essence of what effective managers do. STAR managers take it one step further by developing the keen ability to identify the right time and place for both praise and constructive feedback. Whether it is a big, job-jeopardizing mistake or a small bad habit, coaching opportunities surface constantly.

When coaching your team, there are a number of things you want to do and other practices you want to avoid. The following are the **10 Coaching *Do's*.**

1. **Determine why someone is not succeeding—skill vs. will.** An employee underperforms for one of two reasons: Either he does not know how to properly do his job (skill) or he does not want to put in the hard work to effectively do his job (will). In situations in which an employee lacks will, find ways to motivate him, showing the benefits of working hard. With skill issues, focus on training the employee. The remedy is training or coaching the employee to develop the knowledge to do the job at hand.

2. **Coach for discovery.** A STAR manager does not tell her employee what he is doing wrong. Instead, she asks open-ended questions to help her employee uncover the causes for underperformance on his own. Asking open-ended questions to help employees self-diagnose, such as "Why do you think you aren't meeting expectations?" is much more effective than coming down on your employee and telling him what is wrong. There will be times when your employee does not see his faults, and your questioning can help guide him to the right conclusion. If, for example, it is clear to you that your direct report is not succeeding because he is not paying attention to details, ask him, "What do you do to review your projects before submitting them?" to help him identify the gap.

3. **Use the constructive feedback sandwich.** DOPE managers go right for the kill, stabbing their employees with the things they did wrong. STAR managers realize that the morale of their people must be maintained in the midst of negative feedback. STAR managers use a feedback sandwich. Start with positive feedback, complimenting your employee on an accomplishment or something he does well. Next, clearly point out an area you want him to improve on. Conclude by sandwiching in the negative feedback with some additional positive feedback. Your positive feedback is both substantial and of importance to your employee. There is always a risk of diluting the negative feedback with your compliments, so make sure you get your point across clearly.

Ensure that you are specific in your feedback and that it focuses in something your employee can fix, not just vaguely saying he is a bad employee. The STAR manager goes one step further by helping her employee find possible solutions to the parts of his job he is struggling with.

4. **Be proactive.** Coaching your team is not a passive activity. If you wait too long to coach your team, it may be too late and you will either have to live with the poor results or jump through more hoops (while they produce consistently poor results) to get them fired. Do not let a problem persist by not addressing it.

5. **Put it in context and perspective.** STAR managers help their employees put feedback into context and perspective. There may be only certain situations in which the employee makes a certain mistake (context). At the same time, the feedback you are giving can be either major or minor. If major, help him understand how his actions or attitude will affect his career trajectory and job performance. If the negative feedback is minor, ensure that you are getting your point across but give priority to other feedback or accomplishments.

6. **Use fact-based observations.** Instead of sharing your opinion, offer concrete evidence to back up your coaching content, basing it on observed behavior with examples. If you can speak with concrete evidence instead of emotion, your employee is more likely to improve because he will see your observations as truth instead of opinion. ***Cut through the crap.*** Be aware that most of your people will offer an excuse or rationalization for poor performance. It is important to hear them out, but understand that you will often need to dig deeper to get to the right answer. Don't get caught in the rationalization you are given; instead use a filter to judge its validity.

7. **Document everything.** As discussed in Chapter 5, documentation is a necessary evil for a manager. It is not fun to

do but comes in very handy during coaching opportunities. If you are able to refer to specific situations and specific actions, you will be more effective at convincing your employee of fault, because you have specific evidence to back up your feedback. Keep track of all coaching conversations and the agreed-upon paths forward.

8. **Pick your battles.** A STAR manager knows when to let things go and when to crack down. Deal with a smaller issue that you know will grow and deal with big issues that have a large impact on the team or an individual employee. Tolerate learning errors. Allow your employees to make mistakes and be there to help them learn how to avoid the mistake in the future. When you do let something slide, ensure that you communicate to your team that you know you are letting them get away with it; otherwise they will begin to challenge your authority.

9. **Engage in two-way coaching.** One of the notable differences between STAR managers and DOPE managers is that DOPE managers see coaching as a way to help their direct reports improve. The STAR manager, on the other hand, realizes that effective coaching is a two-way proposition. It can be as easy as asking your employees, "How am I doing as a manager?" or "How can I help you be more successful?" soliciting their suggestions on how you can improve. Asking your employees for genuine feedback is a great way to better understand the areas where you need to improve your skills or find more experience. This not only builds your credibility but also encourages them to value the feedback process. Employees are likely to give you honest feedback in private. Plus, when you seek out, listen to, and change according to feedback you receive, your employees will be inspired to work harder. Moreover, when you ask these questions (if you are doing a good job) it helps your employees reflect and realize what a great boss you are.

10. **Agree on a path forward, monitor, and follow through.** Once you have provided feedback to your employee, it is crucial that you determine a path forward with him and create concrete actions to facilitate improvement that can be measured so that you can track progress. The purpose of coaching is to change behavior and improve results. Without an agreed-upon path forward with clear action steps, your employee is less likely to improve. Then, when your employee is taking steps in the right direction, celebrate progress, or make tweaks if the plan is not working.

There are a number of things that a manager should *not* do when coaching, including the following **3 Coaching *Don'ts*.**

1. **DON'T focus on the person.** DOPE managers make the mistake of attributing a poor result, mistake made, or bad habit to their employee, equating it to a personal flaw. Instead of focusing on the person and his skill deficiencies, focus on the task at hand and the desired result. This changes the focus of the feedback from an employee confrontation to a brainstorming session in which you are teaming together to find a solution.

2. **DON'T openly compare employees.** For those of us with siblings, at some point we have been compared. Our parents would say something like, "Why can't you be like your sister?" If you tell a low-performing employee that she needs to act more like the superstar on your team, she will be unmotivated. Instead of focusing on improving in the areas where she is falling short, she will focus her effort on showing you how her circumstances are different (and more difficult) than the superstar's. Treat each person on your team as an individual when coaching and use the contingency approach to come up with the most appropriate and unique path toward improvement.

3. **DON'T arbitrarily choose a time or place.** When and where you provide coaching is almost as important as the feedback you actually share. STAR managers provide

feedback to employees not only shortly after an applicable incident, but also during a time when the employee is not stressed by a deadline. When you consistently do this, your employees will soon be better at correcting because they will be in the right mindset when receiving feedback. Don't wait; the coaching opportunity will pass or your employee will be less likely to make immediate change. It is also important to provide feedback in a private setting. Your employee will then feel more comfortable sharing insights about issues and it will be easier to construct a path forward in a one-on-one setting.

Remember that having an established relationship, trust, and buy-in are essential for effective coaching. Without this initial step, much of your coaching will be ignored by your employee.

Quick Tip: When coaching an employee, don't sit across the table from him. Sit at the corner of the table near him. In doing this, your body language communicates that you want to tackle this performance issue *with* your employee rather than punish him.

Three Kinds of Coaching Opportunities

There are three main types of coaching opportunities. Each serves its own specific purpose, and STAR managers use all of them to correct unproductive behaviors and improve subpar results. The three types are:

1. Regular, short-term status reviews.

2. Periodic performance reviews.

3. Informal feedback.

Regularly Scheduled, Short-Term Status Sessions

Pre-scheduled, consistently held coaching sessions, often referred to as "one-on-one reviews," are probably the most important coaching opportunity you have with your employees. Whether held weekly, bi-weekly, or monthly, these regular sessions help you identify problem areas faster and allow you to keep a pulse on the improvement (or lack thereof) that an employee makes after receiving coaching. Furthermore, ensuring that you consistently schedule these meetings helps you set time aside that you would normally fill with other job responsibilities.

One-on-one coaching sessions are focused on the shorter term. Think of it as a status meeting in which you get updates, offer course corrections, and provide guidance as to how your employee's smaller actions tie in to his greater job responsibility. The feedback you provide and the topics you cover should be targeted and specific. Besides following the coaching do's and don'ts, during regularly scheduled one-on-ones, focus on providing clear and concise feedback and quickly uncovering whether existing performance issues are due to the level of activity or level of effectiveness. Generally, performance issues arise because your direct report is not putting in enough effort or is focusing effort on the wrong things.

Determining the difference is fairly straightforward. Have your employee walk you through the way he completed his job responsibilities and budgeted his time in the past week. Performance issues will tend to surface. If he is not finishing his most important projects on time, it could be because he has not budgeted enough time to work on them, instead focusing on other job responsibilities. It may also be that out of laziness that he isn't putting in enough effort to complete the projects on time. This walkthrough process will help you uncover the root cause of his performance issues. Then, focus on the path forward, remedying the situation.

Have your employee suggest ideas to improve his performance. Out of the brainstorming, get him to commit to take certain action steps and build a plan with deliverables to solidify the path forward. For example, you might have someone on your team who struggles with facilitating a meeting because he doesn't take enough time to adequately prepare. Help him determine the things he needs to change to improve at meeting facilitation, such as setting aside calendar time 30 minutes beforehand to write out an agenda and notes. Then have your employee commit to setting this time aside and e-mailing you the agenda before any future meeting he leads. This gives you a more formal way to monitor performance.

Along the way, make sure your employee knows the difference between success and failure. With our meeting facilitator, if you set an expectation that "more productive meetings" is the desired result and that you measure success by talking to meeting attendees to get feedback, confirming that 100 percent of them thought the meeting was well run, your employee will be much clearer on what he must do. Then, at future one-on-one sessions (and even between sessions), provide feedback, celebrating progress and constructively advising on how to improve if things remain subpar.

Periodic Performance Reviews

Periodic performance reviews generally occur quarterly or biannually. The scope is broader and a few elements are addressed that are not normally discussed during regularly scheduled one-on-one meetings.

During these sessions, typical topics include performance ratings, possible bonuses or salary changes, and overall accomplishments. Similar to one-on-one coaching sessions, it is important to back up feedback with evidence and allow your employee to weigh in and offer a diagnosis for the drivers behind his performance.

Discuss your employee's strengths and areas for improvement, providing the context that led you to these conclusions. Next, talk about his goals. Recap the goals previously set, discussing progress. Then help him establish (and write down) new goals.

Once you understand his goals, help him understand how he can get from where he is to where he wants to be. Reinforce things he is doing well and suggest ways to mitigate obstacles that would get in the way of achieving his goals. Your ability to discuss both personal and professional goals, as well as ways to support them, is a great example of the amount of trust built between you and your employees.

Always include a career development discussion in performance reviews. Help your employee talk through career aspirations and work with him to solidify what the next steps should be. For those with high aspirations, help them understand the need to go beyond their job responsibilities and give them the opportunity to do so with concrete steps.

Finally, ensure your employees are properly using mentoring to sharpen their skills and learn new things that will help in their careers. Confirm that they are engaging in peer mentoring, helping each other. Secure formal mentors to coach them down the path toward their career goals. And, as always, make sure to collect their feedback on you.

One of the important outputs of an effective performance review, or a separate career development meeting, is a career development plan. As outlined in the first book of the Young Professional's series, ensure that the career blueprint your employee builds includes goals to be achieved, steps to achieve the goals, a set timeframe, ways it will be measured, and a commitment from the employee.

Quick Tip: When making your team goals, don't add "develop our people" at the very end of the list. This makes it seem as though teaching your team is more of an afterthought. If you really feel that developing your people is important, then make it a higher priority.

Informal Feedback

The third and final type of coaching opportunity is informal or ad hoc coaching. These coaching sessions occur outside of regularly scheduled one-on-one sessions and periodic performance reviews, instead occurring when a situation dictates your feedback. These sessions should be direct, and conducted soon after an incident occurs.

When I was managing a sales organization with responsibility for eight states, we struggled with selling a new product set, and I was responsible for driving results. I wanted to determine whether it was a *skill* or *will* situation, so I had all the salespeople who were not selling the product attend a weekly call with me in which I went through their sales funnel of opportunities for this new product. I asked each of them specifics on their customers, coached them on ways to improve how they positioned the product with customers, and got them to commit to take certain actions with each opportunity. Every salesperson falling short of expectation had to sit on the call; upwards of 40 people who hadn't yet sold enough of the product read out their status.

Some managers would stop at collecting this info and discussing the new product sales opportunities on the call, but I followed up. During subsequent calls, I asked each person about what he or she did for a specific opportunity, referencing the customer by name. If the employee hadn't made progress, it was clear he or she wasn't focused on selling this product.

Not wanting to be embarrassed in front of their peers, people soon started taking action, and the number of people who needed to be on the call got smaller and smaller. In a short amount of time, we became the best region in the entire country at selling this new product.

STAR managers know that if they follow up on areas their employees have committed to improving, then their employees are more likely to improve.

When coaching your team, it is important to understand that not everyone will be open to feedback. Besides providing excuses, they may be argumentative, passing blame to you, another work group, or some uncontrollable circumstance. Don't be discouraged. When you are persistent, fair, and clear about your feedback, your employee will know that you won't give up, and he will either improve or find another role better suited for his skills and interests.

Performance Improvement Plans

Whether dealing with coaching difficult employees, yes men, or roller-coaster riders, or when your coaching does not produce immediate results, there will be times when you have to put your employees on performance improvement plans (PIPs).

Most companies have unique names for this kind of document (to hide the severity of what it really is), but in reality it is a document that outlines how an employee must improve, spelling out the goals he must reach and the actions he must take or he will get fired.

Remember that your ultimate success in business is not what *you* do but what you can get *others* to do. A STAR manager is able to get her people to performer better than a DOPE manager can though effectively leveraging coaching and feedback, focusing on specific ways employees can improve. STAR managers understand that just as a chain is only as strong as its weakest link, a team is only as strong as its weakest performer.

> *Don't measure yourself by what you have accomplished, but by what you should have accomplished with your ability.*
> —John Wooden

> *Talent is the multiplier. The more energy and attention you invest in it, the greater the yield. The time you spend with your best is, quite simply, your most productive time.*
> —Marcus Buckingham

The STAR Manager vs. The DOPE Manager

The DOPE manager views coaching as a means to terminate employees. He offers little assistance beyond exposing employee issues and criticizing methods.

The STAR manager uses coaching to help employees improve. Besides uncovering skill vs. will issues, she guides her direct reports down a pathway to improvement, consistently addressing issues head-on instead of letting employees continue to fail.

Explore Online: On TheSparkSource.com Resources page you will find the "One-on-One Review Worksheet" and the "Performance Review Worksheet," which will help guide you through the process of coaching and giving feedback to your employees.

CHAPTER 13

Empowering Your Team: Motivation Is the Fuel of Peak Performance

What to Expect: The ability to motivate employees to go above and beyond what their job requires is a central skill to being an effective young manager. In this chapter, we'll discuss how to motivate employees, how to connect your goals and vision with theirs, and how to convert motivation into empowerment.

Management is nothing more than motivating other people.

—Lee Iacocca

People often say motivation doesn't last. Neither does bathing—that's why we recommend it daily.
  —Zig Ziglar

Things weren't going well.

It seemed that the typical ways I guided a team to success weren't working. I put together new strategies, created an improved team recognition program, and even worked with the team to roll out a new training initiative, but nothing seemed to change our negative trajectory. Although I didn't like the idea of having to use negativity, it was my last option.

I don't consider myself to be much of a "rah-rah" kind of manager, but I had to light a fire under my team to get us moving. As I walked into my weekly team meeting, I knew it was time to put on a show.

I started the meeting by reviewing results, pointing out how far behind our goals we were but showing my optimism that we could turn things around. I started a brainstorming discussion on how we could dig ourselves out of this hole when BOOM, excuses and poor attitudes appeared. It was time for me to let loose. *And...action!*

"This is ridiculous!" I shouted. "What is going on with everyone? We are better than this. We have done it before and we can do this again. We need to change. Stop complaining and coming up with excuses! I have offered up every idea I have and you all aren't doing anything about it!"

As I looked across the conference room at my team, all I saw were blank faces and eyes staring at me, dumbfounded. Offering the knock-out punch I exclaimed, "That's it. I can't take this. You guys figure this out!" and I pushed a few chairs out of the way in frustration as I stormed out of the room and down the hall. I proceeded to go for a walk outside, offering the team time to think about what had happened.

I later found out that after sitting there for a couple minutes, the team started to rally together. They saw more clearly that they had begun believing they couldn't reach our goals, which in reality they knew were achievable. Luckily, my strategy worked. The team realized that they were too caught up in the frustration of not performing up to our potential and now understood we had to adapt to be successful. From then on, the team stopped complaining and instead focused on the goals ahead, working to find creative ways to improve performance.

When I first started as a manager, I was very conscious of my duty to motivate the people I managed. However, I was scared and didn't think I really knew how to motivate anyone but myself to accomplish anything. In time, I realized that managers have an incredible impact on the performance of their team, and motivation is the most impactful tool in affecting individual and team performance.

At its core, motivation comes from belief.

My employees had stopped believing they could succeed. In doing this, they were less motivated to focus, work hard, and take steps to achieve our goals. While effective managers leverage motivation as a tool, STAR managers go one step further. They *empower* their people.

By definition, empowerment is about enablement while motivation only involves giving someone a reason to act a certain way (in other words, a "motive"), inciting them to action. When you empower people, you give *them* the power and authority to achieve. Generally, motivation comes from external sources. It can come from a boss, a situation, or even the idea of achieving a goal. Empowerment, on the other hand, is self-generated. It develops when someone believes deeply in what she is doing and is strengthened when she knows achieving her goals is possible. A STAR manager understands how to show her employees that they have the ability to develop their own internal desire to achieve goals.

While motivation is communicated by you in a way *you* think will excite your employees, empowerment is the way your employees translate the message to truly engage and focus *themselves* on the goals at hand. Empowerment is more lasting. Motivation is a first step, and the internalization of external motivation (empowerment) is the next, when the motivation you give your employees truly sticks and becomes ingrained in who they are professionally.

How to Turn Motivation Into Empowerment

Here are 15 ways that STAR managers empower their employees. It's not necessary to master all of them, but targeted use of these tactics can foster employee empowerment.

1. **The carrot vs. the stick.** Motivation comes in two forms: positive and negative. Threats of a punishment can get you short-term results and temporary motivation, but fear is not empowering. "The stick" strategy will lead your team to break rules when you aren't looking and requires you to be the constant task-master. "The carrot," or showing your team the positive outcomes of following your vision, is lasting and can more easily translate to empowerment.

2. **Set your employees up for success.** Align people with their strengths. Employees tend to have more confidence when they believe they will do a good job. This confidence grows when they feel their role is closely aligned with their strengths. It is important to challenge your employees and give them opportunities outside of their comfort zone, allowing them to use and perfect their strengths.

3. **Repeat your encouraging messages.** To properly internalize motivation and translate it into empowerment, your employees must consistently hear messages affirming that they can accomplish their goals. A STAR manager consistently reminds her team until they believe it.

4. **Connect your goals and vision with theirs.** When people see the personal benefit they receive from striving for a goal, there is a higher likelihood that they will be empowered to work until achieving it. Find out what is important to your employees and show how achieving the team's goals and

vision will lead them to achieve their own goals. Leverage simplicity. If you complicate your team's jobs by creating too many competing priorities or too many rules, it will be harder for them to know the right focal point for their effort.

5. **Explain the importance of the work they do.** People feel more fulfilled when they believe the work they do really matters. STAR managers are masters at tying the role and goals of the team with those of the greater organization, giving the team a sense that their role is substantial.

6. **Pay attention to your employees.** Effective managers understand that they must pay attention to their employees. DOPE managers work in parallel with their teams, focusing on their own projects and own success, while STAR managers show their employees they are valuable by paying attention to them, their work, and their professional development.

7. **Be empathetic.** A STAR manager shows her team that she understands the challenges of her employees' jobs. She pictures herself in their shoes, not only to show that she cares, but also to help her have the right frame of mind when making decisions. This recognition of your team and the life they live at work each day motivates them to succeed.

8. **Teach your people.** As mentioned in Chapter 5, when you help your team learn and develop, they will feel more fulfilled in their job and more engaged in what they are doing. STAR managers know that knowledge empowers, and they build learning opportunities into everyday work situations both formally (through special educational sessions) and informally when a lesson arises.

9. **Use creativity.** The same old day-to-day can bore your team. Anything you can do to spice up the normal monotony of their job can help engage and motivate your team. Your simple creative ideas to recognize, teach, or support your employees will pay dividends. The team will feel comfortable with showing their own creativity as well.

10. **Maintain open lines of communication.** Communicating what is happening in the organization, especially things that will affect your team's jobs, is a tool STAR managers use to motivate. As John Zenger and Joseph Folkman assert in their book *The Extraordinary Leader*, the best managers establish open lines of communication and regularly ask empowering questions like, "What are you getting that you want? What are you getting that you do not want? What are you not getting?"

11. **Give responsibility, impact, and the freedom to act.** Beyond just *telling* your team they have impact, give them the opportunity to actually *have* impact. Giving your employees responsibility and a chance to control an outcome empowers and engages them. This involves giving up some control and trusting your team. The feeling of being trusted with something important and impactful motivates and gives employees a sense of purpose and confidence in their own abilities, translating to empowerment.

12. **Allow your employees to give input.** Don't just stop at communicating *why* things happen in a certain way. Leveraging your team's expertise and experience not only helps you make more educated decisions, but also motivates your team to follow through with the directives you give because they feel as though they are part of the process.

13. **Create a positive work environment.** A STAR manager realizes that her actions are not the only way to empower her employees. While a DOPE manager may lead toward authoritarian decisions and selfishly taking the spotlight, a STAR manager creates an environment where her people feel their opinions are valued, their work is impactful, and they have a sense of control of their results.

14. **Allow your employees to make mistakes.** People feel less empowered to take action and follow through when they fear they will be penalized for failure. Allowing risk and treating failure as a learning experience further facilitates

this. Instead of constricting your team to limit the chance for failure, realize that failure is where the best career lessons are born. Have a plan to manage, monitor, and anticipate failure, but allow your entire team to learn from each other's mistakes.

15. **Motivate the individual.** STAR managers don't just focus on empowering the team as a whole, but also know that motivating *the individual* better translates to empowerment. Each of your employees has a separate set of goals, diverse expertise, and different methods of achieving. The language in which motivation translates into empowerment is very different for each of your direct reports.

Quick Tip: Tell your team that they are #1. If you constantly remind them that they are the best team, they will live up to this expectation. Then uphold a standard that your team must act as though they are the best already. If you act as if it is okay not to be #1, then you will begin to accept mediocrity.

When You Don't Empower

A lack of motivation is a cancer for the team and causes several undesired effects. Without motivation, people scatter, losing their focus on the team and becoming only concerned with themselves. Soon the quality of work drops as a lack of engagement flourishes. This translates to a rise in DOPE behavior, from lack of self-awareness to poor results. Ultimately, the team's top talent begins to look for new opportunities outside of the team, eventually leaving.

In the *Harvard Business Review* article "The Set-Up-to-Fail Syndrome," Jean-Francois Manzoni and Jean-Louis Barsoux point out that much of an employee's motivation comes from how his manager views him. If you start to perceive your employees as unmotivated, then they will be "less motivated, less energetic, and less likely to go beyond the call of duty." This leads them to be "less innovative and less likely to suggest ideas." Your management style has an enormous effect. Not motivating your employees creates a snowball effect that negatively affects all aspects of the team.

Why Empowerment Is Important

There are a number of reasons why empowering your people is a valuable tool.

1. **Influence and direction.** When you motivate your team to rally around a shared direction and vision, then you are able to get the group to achieve great things. Empowerment is born out of having a clear vision and belief in the goals for which the team is striving.

2. **Building morale.** When an employee is empowered, he is happier at work and buys in to a positive team culture. This creates a contagious effect, empowering the entire team and improving everyone's overall confidence and positive outlook.

3. **Creating momentum.** The STAR manager knows that when she empowers an employee's mindset changes, she creates a snowball effect such that the success of each team member builds on the last and the team achieves exponentially more. The positive morale creates momentum.

4. **Fostering team engagement.** In the book *The Power of Full Engagement*, authors Jim Loehr and Tony Schwartz note that managing energy and not time is what creates engagement. This engagement is rooted in being empowered, and engagement is even more important for our peer Millennials who become easily bored; empowerment engages.

5. **Making it about the team.** To motivate your team and help translate this motivation to internally driven empowerment, you have to focus on the team unit and each individual. Moreover, good leaders are able to build successful teams

while they are present, but great leaders develop people who perform at the highest level long after they are gone. The way leaders create this lasting effect is by empowering their employees.

6. **Generating initiative and innovation.** Empowerment leads the team to show more initiative and innovation, taking action through new and creative methods. Once their peers start to take this positive action, the entire team is inspired to take action as well, knowing that they make an impact. This empowerment then leads people to take ownership of their jobs and finally manifests itself when your employees successfully enact a variety of STAR attributes.

When You Empower

When you foster an environment of empowerment, ***you develop and retain your top talent.*** STAR managers use empowerment to make their top employees (and every other employee) feel valued and contribute true impact. STAR managers recognize and reward them, challenge them, and give them their own time and focus, communicating that they are important.

Remember that effective motivation translates to empowerment when a manager creates the proper environment. STAR managers don't just focus on the team as a unit but realize that each employee speaks a different empowerment language.

A good leader inspires people to have confidence in the leader; a great leader inspires people to have confidence in themselves.

—Anonymous

The STAR Manager vs. The DOPE Manager

The DOPE manager inappropriately threatens employees to get them to improve so they avoid consequence. He sees money as the primary driver for employee engagement and dangles it in front of employees to get better results.

The STAR manager not only motivates employees, but creates an environment where this motivation is internalized and converts into empowerment, leading her team members to proactively take action and move closer to attaining goals.

CHAPTER 14

Removing Obstacles: The Overlooked Role of a Manager

What to Expect: Removing obstacles is an often forgotten job responsibility that separates managers with recurring team problems from those who consistently succeed amidst adversity. This chapter addresses how to remove obstacles and handle situations in which obstacles can't be removed, without defocusing employees.

The goal of management is to remove obstacles.
—Paul Orfalea

From the hack, the thrower starts the delivery, pushing the stone across the sheet toward the house, past the center line, trying to land on the button.

To most, this sounds like a foreign language, but it is a reality to a very small subset of athletes.

That's right, we are talking about curling. Although curling is not widely understood and is often made fun of, as it's like a giant game of shuffleboard on ice, the sport provides an interesting illustration of effective management. In curling, the thrower or "curler" pushes a giant circular stone on the ice toward a target at the other end of the playing surface. Once the curler lets go, a group of sweepers using brooms sweep a few inches ahead of the moving stone. The sweepers' main purpose is to remove the ice in front of the traveling stone, reducing friction underneath the stone and better controlling its direction while it is spinning.

Just as the sweepers prepare the way for the curler's stone, removing obstacles that may slow it down, a manager's job is to smooth the way for her team to succeed, removing obstacles that slow down team members from doing their jobs.

The responsibility of removing obstacles is often forgotten by managers; responsibilities like coaching and motivating being at the forefront of their minds. STAR managers understand the importance of removing barriers and know that when they effectively remove these roadblocks, team morale increases and performance improves.

Put differently, removing these hindrances proves to your team that you are their advocate. Creating this sense that you "have their backs" is a key step STAR managers know they need to guide their team to peak performance.

Obstacles come in many forms. Essentially, barriers are things that prevent the team from performing optimally. They can take the shape of a process the team must follow or a policy that dictates certain steps must be taken. It may also take the form of a conflict within the team or a circumstance that you and the team may or may not have any control over.

Additional examples of obstacles include: bottlenecks in systems that slow down your team, job requirements or steps that are time-wasters, re-work that the team must do, overlapping processes such that multiple people or groups perform the same step in a process, unnecessary steps, exceptions that need approval, and a lack of freedom or authority to make decisions.

When I managed a call center that wrote services orders for our top enterprise customers, I routinely had to expedite orders to have the services installed earlier than the standard installation date to meet customer demands. The fact that my people often did not have the authority to get other departments to expedite an order required that they escalate the situation to me so that I could get the request moved up. These would generally involve me calling a peer manager in another department (or possibly escalating further to their boss) to ensure an exception could be made. This became an almost daily norm, but my quick turnaround time on these expedites removed a large barrier for my team and showed them that I was their advocate.

A great way to uncover these obstacles is through the "venting session" in team meetings when your direct reports have the opportunity to complain about issues. Another effective forum for learning about new obstacles is in feedback and coaching sessions. The STAR manager offers her analysis and advice to her employee and then asks for feedback on the things that are making her employee's job harder than it should be, so that she knows what obstacles to focus on eliminating or mitigating.

Make sure that the obstacles you uncover are vetted with the team so you identify the stumbling blocks you can remove that have the greatest impact on the team. As mentioned, when someone comes to you and says that "everyone" thinks a certain issue is a big barrier, this does not mean that everyone really feels this is an issue you should pursue fixing; it may just be one person bringing it up. At the same time, removing a big obstacle for a certain employee may be worth the effort, because it could catapult him from poor results to great results.

Why Removing Obstacles Is Important

There are a number of reasons why removing obstacles is an important function of a manager, including:

1. **It keeps the team focused.** Obstacles are distractions. They take your employees away from effectively doing their jobs and generally permeate the rest of the team. Talk about struggles travels like wildfire before everyone starts to see the issues and how they affect their jobs. Removing obstacles allows the team to focus solely on doing their job.

2. **It creates momentum.** A team with an absence of big barriers is a team free to achieve their goals. Besides being a distraction, obstacles are momentum killers because work is either drawn out or your employees must regularly start again and stop again.

3. **It increases job satisfaction.** Obstacles cause frustration and lower morale. People tend to feel more like they are fighting fires and dealing with unfamiliar situations when obstacles arise. As problems become routine, they begin to wear on people. By removing these obstacles, your employees can do better-quality work that is ultimately more satisfying.

4. **Obstacles won't go away on their own.** The DOPE manager becomes aware of an issue and then decides to sweep it under the rug, pushing responsibility for fixing it to someone else. A STAR manager, on the other hand, takes initiative because she knows how barriers adversely affect her team and that they won't go away unless she takes ownership and ensures they are solved.

5. **It helps you succeed in adversity.** When leading in a constant state of change as most managers today must do, you have to use the existence of obstacles to your advantage. It is impossible to remove every obstacle your team faces, but when you are able to remove some of the more disruptive ones, the team has more confidence that they can succeed in the face of adversity. They are also encouraged to follow through, knowing that you are working hard to make things easier for them, and recognizing that they must overcome obstacles in the meantime.

Quick Tip: When escalating an issue for an employee, use the deadline rule. Inform the other party you are escalating with that if they don't solve their part of the issue by a set time, then you will escalate to their boss. This generally gets people to do their jobs and helps you remove an obstacle faster.

How to Remove Obstacles

In many cases, uncovering obstacles is not much of a challenge and can be as simple as asking your team a question. Skill comes into play once you collect the list of barriers, and then work to remove them. Here is an outline of the mindset to develop and the steps to take in order to remove obstacles and free your team from issues so they can succeed:

1. **Leave your ego at the door.** To be effective at removing obstacles, you must be willing to get your hands dirty. Eliminating these issues can be one of the toughest parts of your job. By having an attitude that you will go to any lengths to remove obstacles for your team, you will gain their respect. Even when you aren't able to navigate around a barrier, they will be more willing to work hard through it.

2. **Collect and understand issues first.** Besides being willing to ask what the issues are, STAR managers probe to get to the true root of a problem. Instead of just accepting a challenge your team vocalizes, probe to understand it fully so that you can investigate the best pathways for a solution.

3. **Take on the burden for the team.** A STAR manager takes on the burden of eliminating obstacles for her employees so that the team can continue to focus on doing their day-to-day jobs. Be very clear that you are taking responsibility but, at the same time, engage them to help with steps in the process if you aren't able to resolve the issue on your own.

4. **Get creative and innovate with solutions.** There are often better ways to do things than the current way. Brainstorm

a variety of different solutions that could fix the issue you have committed to fixing and think through how each option would benefit the affected stakeholders (your employees, your boss, your peers, your customers, and yourself).

5. **Lift the obstacles to the higher-ups.** Once you have collected the issues and developed a number of creative alternatives, approach your boss (or whomever the appropriate party would be) and speak to him about the obstacles your team has identified, sharing the negative impact it has on your team's results. Then introduce the various suggested solutions to gain support for the one that everyone agrees is the best option.

6. **Don't forget the small obstacles.** Eliminating big obstacles is very important and generally has the greatest effect on the team; however, removing smaller obstacles can also be motivating and engaging. I once managed a team that felt that there was an employee in the office (who worked for a peer of mine) who talked very loudly in his cubicle when on the phone, thereby distracting and annoying everyone around him. I spoke to the loud employee's manager, and we came up with a solution that didn't disrupt her employee but that allowed my team and others sitting around him to work in peace and quiet. Solving that issue took next to no time or effort on my part, but meant a great deal to my team.

7. **Consider short-term versus long-term solutions.** When solving problems and removing barriers, ensure that you consider both the long- and short-term consequences of your remedy. There are times when a quick fix only temporarily solves an issue instead of permanently eliminating it. The STAR manager ensures that her solutions resolve issues for the long term so they do not continually disrupt her team, but also leverages short-term solutions when merited.

8. **Follow through.** DOPE managers may be good at collecting a list of obstacles but then let the process end there, never actually removing the obstacle for their team. The real

focus should not be on uncovering issues but instead resolving them.

9. **Build an ecosystem.** In almost every case, you will need to engage others to help you remove an obstacle your team is facing. Help may come in the form of your boss, a peer, individuals on your team, other departments, external entities like suppliers or other vendors, and even your customers. It is important to build a network of these resources that can help you. Whereas you may serve as the coordinator to resolve an issue, you will need an ecosystem of others to assist.

Immovable Obstacles

There will be times when even your best efforts to remove a hindrance will end in failure. This is a reality, given that there are a number of things you can't control. In these cases, it is best to keep your team from becoming unfocused.

When you are not able to follow through on resolving an issue, or you find that there is no solution, it is best to be upfront and honest that this is the case. Share with your team the steps you took to find a solution, and they will respect the genuine effort you put forth.

In these situations, remind your team of the obstacles that you *have* succeeded in removing and the ones they have overcome. Assure them that you will continue to work hard to eliminate future issues your team brings to your attention. Then, engage the team to brainstorm best practices for dealing with the obstacle. Don't downplay the issue completely, as this can alienate your employees, but focus on alternatives and potential ways to cope with an obstacle instead of dwelling on it.

Although it often isn't glamorous work, removing obstacles for your team is one of the most impactful things STAR managers do that most other managers don't proactively think about. Be willing to pick up a broom and start sweeping ahead of the stone for your curler (a.k.a. your employee). You are right there on the ice with them and are in the best position to smooth out the surface ahead so that their efforts can travel farther.

The rock that is an obstacle in the path of one person becomes a stepping-stone in the path of another.

—Unknown

The STAR Manager vs. The DOPE Manager

The DOPE manager is great at identifying obstacles but sees them as things that are out of his control, so he conditions his team to accept them as realities of the job. When he does make an effort to remove an obstacle, he stops fighting for his team if he receives any pushback, explaining to his team that he "tried."

The STAR manager pushes aside her ego and rolls up her sleeves to do anything to make her team succeed. She sees that one of her primary responsibilities is to remove obstacles that stand in the way of her team reaching its full potential.

CHAPTER 15

Team Recognition:
The Power of Saying *Thank You*

What to Expect: Everyone likes their accomplishments to be recognized, but in diverse ways. Some are fine with just a pat on the back behind closed doors whereas others want public recognition, complete with pomp and circumstance. This chapter presents the benefits of recognition and how to develop and implement a recognition plan to better motivate your employees toward maximum performance.

Some people feel they work in an environment where doing a good job is like wetting your pants in a dark suit...it gives you a warm feeling but nobody notices!
—Grant M. Bright

Catch people doing things right.
—Ken Blanchard

"And the winner of this month's 'Data Diamond' award is... Stephanie!" A round of applause ensued while Stephanie came up to the front of the room to accept her certificate and the diamond traveling trophy.

Each month, the Data Diamond award was the most sought-after recognition I had created for my team to help us focus on selling our portfolio of data products, something we had struggled with, and an area my boss had really been pushing the organization to improve upon. Each month, whoever sold the most data products or was the most improved at selling them received the award. Even though our office only had touch-down stations, instead of dedicated desks or cubicles, I made sure to showcase the trophy and post the monthly certificate on the front side of my cubicle so that everyone in the office could see it when they walked by. The Data Diamond award was a simple form of recognition. It only took me a couple minutes a month to choose the winner and print the certificate, but it drastically improved results: we saw a 1,200-percent increase in the sales of the data product set.

Recognizing and thanking your team for their accomplishments and hard work is something that STAR managers master. The potential for rewards is a valuable motivating factor that entices employees to put forth their best effort and buy in to team goals.

The DOPE manager believes that a monetary reward is the only true motivator, whereas the STAR manager knows that recognition comes in many forms. For STAR managers, recognition includes:

☆ Bonuses, raises, and other monetary rewards.

☆ Exposure to senior leaders in your organization.

☆ Certificates, ribbons, or trophies denoting an accomplishment or specific award.

☆ Letters or other forms of written appreciation.

☆ Public sharing of accomplishments.

☆ Additional job responsibilities or authority.

☆ Time off or some form of work flexibility or freedom.

☆ Formalized development programs or mentoring.

☆ Gifts or meals.

☆ Team parties or social functions.

☆ Events, including performing arts or sports.

☆ A pat on the back and a vocal thank-you.

Your recognition programs should be a combination of company- or organization-sponsored programs (helping your team focus their efforts on achieving what leadership wants them to) and rewards that you create for your team. Often the forms of recognition *you* initiate mean more to the team and foster greater empowerment.

Don't be afraid to spend your time or bring out your wallet to reward your team. DOPE managers flinch at the thought of paying their own money to thank their teams. STAR managers know it is because of their team's hard work that they earn paychecks, bonuses, and raises.

> **Quick Tip:** Some of the most effective forms of recognition are simple. The best thing you can say to an employee who has worked really hard is "I'm proud of you."

Regardless of the form your recognition takes, there are **two rules** a STAR manager upholds when thanking her team:

☆ **1st Rule of Recognition:** *When the result is bad, take the blame and responsibility to improve things. When results are positive, give the credit to the team.* All rewards should be focused on your team and its individual members. A STAR manager offers no sense that she deserves credit. She knows that her team earned any award bestowed upon her and acknowledges the team. Whenever I receive an award or recognition that my team helped me earn, I credit them. There are a number of certificates in my office crediting an award to "Aaron McDaniel." In these cases I cover up the word Aaron with the word "Team," so that it reads "Team McDaniel." It may seem like a minor change, but it represents a huge shift not only in my mindset but also in the eyes of my team, who recognize that I value the accomplishment they earned for me. As Richard Elder eloquently states in his book *If I Knew Then What I Know Now,* "The way to receive a lot of recognition and credit is to give away as much of it as possible."

☆ **2nd Rule of Recognition:** *Recognize the right things.* STAR managers are careful about what they recognize, knowing that recognition and rewards perpetuate behavior. In *On Folly of Rewarding A, While Hoping for B,* Steven Kerr accurately characterizes how we must align what we want with the rewards we give. If we want to foster more teamwork but reward individuals, then our recognition is misaligned. If you demand quality but measure speed, or want long-term success but only reward short-term gains, you have a suboptimal recognition program. Align what you recognize with your goals. Link rewards to performance and use them to reinforce key principles and desired behaviors.

A number of elements contribute to creating a powerful recognition program. STAR managers are able to balance diverse factors, knowing that recognition is a tool to guide their teams to achieving stated goals. Effective recognition is:

1. **Short-term and long-term.** STAR managers recognize their employees for both short-term success and long-term accomplishment. It is important to balance both so that your direct reports don't focus on just one scope of time.

2. **Spontaneous and set.** Rewards should be both set, so that the team can have an end goal to strive for and look forward to, and unexpected, so that there is an element of surprise. In *The Prince,* Machiavelli explained that established

recognition becomes an expectation and therefore can lose some effectiveness, whereas spontaneous and unanticipated rewards encourage your people to always work hard because there is a possibility for recognition at any moment.

3. **Group and individual.** Effective managers find ways to recognize the team through group rewards, such as team outings, to reinforce how important the team unit is and that everyone must help each other. One effective strategy to encourage this behavior and recognize the team is to offer a prize if *each person* meets a certain requirement—not just the overall team average. Simultaneously recognize individuals so that lower-performing team members can see appropriate behaviors while higher performers feel appreciated.

4. **Small and big wins.** Big wins, such as reaching an annual goal, are fairly easy to track and common to recognize. Although it is imperative to recognize such major accomplishments, STAR managers also keep an eye out for small accomplishments. Recognizing baby steps is a great way to coach employees and reinforce positives changes and proper behaviors. Recognizing small wins also helps break down large and complex goals into small pieces, guiding the team to the next step in achieving their vision.

5. **Public and private.** As the saying goes, "reward in public, discipline in private." Some people get more job satisfaction and reinforcement when their peers hear about their accomplishments in a public setting. Public recognition also further communicates the right behaviors for those not performing well, fostering a healthy sense of competition. It is also important, however, to recognize or reward in private. Thanking an employee behind closed doors and explaining that you view them as unique among their peers can be just as reassuring as a public display of appreciation.

6. **Customized to the individual.** People like to be recognized in different ways. Some people like huge displays of appreciation, fanfare, and trophies, whereas others prefer a

private pat on the back. Some prefer words, others want a physical award, and still others are motivated by a sense of accomplishment. It is important to understand how each of your direct reports likes to be recognized. This is one of the primary reasons why "How do you like to be recognized?" is one of the most important questions to ask your employees during your first one-on-one meeting.

7. **Consistent and fair.** A STAR manager knows that if one person is recognized, she needs to offer a similar form of recognition to others. Moreover, she finds ways to level the playing field. In order not to discourage lower-performing employees, she institutes recognition plans that reward things like improvement and not just overall achievement.

8. **Formal and informal.** Effective recognition is a mixture of formal, established rewards that have established processes, such as organization-wide awards, and informal awards, when your direct reports can recognize each other, such as having "shout-outs."

9. **Done personally.** STAR managers involve themselves in the process. As employee motivation expert Bob Nelson recommends, personally thank people face-to-face and in writing, early, often, and sincerely. If you want to thank an employee who works in another office, go to his office and thank him in person. Be willing to offer yourself as a form of recognition. In the past, I have done tasks that my employees dislike doing as a way to recognize their accomplishment.

10. **Genuine.** People see through disingenuous recognition and fake thank-yous. Genuine recognition is more than just surface-level; it is deep and lasting. Proper recognition is given when people know they deserve it.

11. **Appropriate and proportional.** The bigger or more significant the accomplishment, the larger the reward should be. If you offer a huge award for something insignificant, it may be hard to sustain when everyone begins to accomplish it; if you offer a small reward for a big accomplishment, people won't be motivated to strive for it.

12. **Creative.** Recognition can tend toward the boring and repetitious. STAR managers use their creativity to offer unique rewards. For example, on each of my employees' birthdays, I give them their favorite candy as a thank-you. At the end of each year, I come up with creative awards custom-made for each direct report. For example, I would give a "Best Hair" award to someone with unique hairdos, a "Power Walker" award to someone who liked to take walks during lunch break, and the "Straight Talk" award to someone who speaks his mind with the team. Even today, a number of my past employees have kept and display these certificates.

13. **Simple.** Don't make your recognition methods too complicated. A simple "thank you" can go a long way. Moreover, the more rules a contest has or the more exceptions or complexities involved in winning an award, the less engaged and motivated your team will be to work toward earning it.

14. **Specific.** Don't just say "thank you" generically; specify what you are thanking your employee for. Doing this will increase the likelihood that the employee (and your other employees) will perpetuate the right behaviors. Recognition is more meaningful when you describe exactly what your employee accomplished.

15. **Put in the best light.** STAR managers make their employees sound as impressive as possible. STAR managers play up their employees to their peer managers and their boss. They also find the right terms to communicate the accomplishment. For example, if you have someone who moved his request-processing time from one hour to 30 minutes, talk about how he improved his processing time by 50 percent.

16. **Used as a learning experience.** STAR managers make recognition a time to share best practices so the whole team can improve. Instead of just congratulating an employee for his accomplishment in front of the team, have him share *how* he accomplished his goal or won an award so that the rest of the team can grow and develop.

17. **Team-decided.** Most of the forms of recognition managers implement come from themselves or the organization they are a part of, but it is valuable to have some rewards that are determined by the team. When the team chooses their own recognition, they will be more inclined to work hard to accomplish it, because (A) the reward is something they actually want, and (B) they think the goal is achievable.

18. **Just because.** An effective form of recognition is rewarding your team just because they are your team. These forms of recognition foster deeper group relationships and solidify bonds. When managing a call center team, I baked cookies or brownies for my team to enjoy during team meetings. This was something simple that led my team to be more engaged and motivated, just because I was their manager.

19. **Fun.** Instead of making your forms of recognition boring, spice them up. I have done everything from taking my team indoor skydiving to go-kart racing. As long as it is considered fun by the team (not just you) and is work-appropriate, then it can be effective.

20. **Sought-after.** Rewards should be exclusive. If everyone had them, people will not work as hard to earn them. Additionally, the rewards should be something that people care about. For example, AT&T has an annual award called Diamond Club that recognizes the top 1 percent of salespeople. Winners receive a free trip for two (the year I won, the group went to Hawaii), as well as other prizes. As managers, we do not have the resources to offer such an extravagant reward on our own, but we can determine the right reward and thresholds that will motivate our employees to put forth their maximum effort.

Quick Tip: Remember to thank and recognize yourself. Reward yourself from time to time and keep reminders of when others thank you. I keep a "thank you" folder in my e-mail so that I have a place to go when I need cheering up.

Benefits of Recognition

Recognizing your employees pays many dividends. Besides increasing results, it motivates your employees and helps to transform motivation into empowerment. Proper recognition engages your direct reports and, when the rewards are properly aligned, it focuses them on the goals you want them to achieve.

Effective recognition creates a sense of community. In their writings, Jim Kouzes and Barry Posner note that when you get together to reinforce shared principles, it creates community because extraordinary accomplishment is the result of the efforts of many. This recognition establishes a sense of appreciation among the team.

Remember to give credit freely and reward the right things. This creates a healthy team environment and offers your employees a clear benefit for working hard and achieving team goals.

> *A ruler should be slow to punish and swift to reward.*
> —Ovid

> *Most people do not receive nearly enough appreciation. How can this be when appreciation is free, easy, and readily available? All you have to do is speak. Go give some away now.*
> —Rhoberta Shaler

The STAR Manager vs. The DOPE Manager

The DOPE manager takes credit when good things happen and skirts blame. He doesn't augment company recognition programs with his own and is selfish about giving up his own money to recognize his team's efforts.

The STAR manager says "thank you" often. She takes more than her share of the blame and less than her share of the credit, instead recognizing the efforts of her team and rewarding STAR behavior by her employees. She celebrates big and small wins and tailors the recognition to the person being recognized.

CHAPTER 16

Guiding the Old and the Young: Managing People of Different Generations

What to Expect: Currently there are three generations within the workforce. As a young manager, you will be put in situations in which you have to manage people of all ages. STAR managers recognize the differences in communication and working styles of different generations and leverage the various strengths of each generation to help the team. This chapter offers strategies on how to manage people from all generations.

A great person attracts great people and knows how to hold them together.

—Johann Wolfgang Von Goethe

179

Authority without wisdom is like a heavy axe without an edge, fitter to bruise than polish.

—Anne Bradstreet

Harry was in his mid 60s, had grandkids, and was pretty set in his ways. I was a young manager in my 20s, eager to turn around an underperforming team. When I sat down with Harry to hold my typical introductory "get to know you" initial one-on-one meeting, he boldly took control.

"Let me share with you an analogy. Here is the mountain," Harry asserted, angling his arm in a parabolic sloping motion. "Here is you," he explained, using his fingers to walk up the front side of the imaginary hill, "and here I am," he continued, jumping his walking fingers down the bottom of the back side of his fictitious mountain. "I'm already 'over the hill.' I will work hard and put forth my best effort, but I am on my way out. As long as you understand this analogy, things will work between us," he concluded, chuckling.

Harry and I were in very different places in our careers. He was of the Baby Boomer generation, and just looking to get a paycheck so he could spend time with his family, travel, and finish paying off the house he had bought 20 years prior. I was just starting out, itching to make my mark and work 24/7 if I needed to, in order to reach my goals. We went through some growing pains and misunderstandings as we built a working relationship with each other, but in time I learned how to leverage Harry's strengths and experience while he accepted my youthful enthusiasm, periodic naivety, and new management methods, and he rallied behind my team vision.

The ability to manage a diverse workforce is a valuable skill that STAR managers develop as they learn how to bridge differences and utilize varying opinions and levels of experience to enable their team to perform better. In my career, I have managed people my age, some younger than me, and even some who had worked at my company longer than I had been alive. In each unique situation, I leveraged these STAR manager concepts and the mindset outlined in this chapter with notable results.

Today's workforce is primarily a melting pot of Baby Boomers, Gen Xers, and Millennials, from a plethora of ethnic and national backgrounds. Whereas some may shy away from the complexities this creates, we Millennials have grown up with the propensity to value and learn from these diversities.

Embracing these diversities is even more important as a young manager. If you don't have the right mindset, factions will develop within your team, people will feel misunderstood, and ultimately your team will become disengaged and unmotivated.

Because of age diversity, it is even more important for you to maintain a contingency approach to management, or you face the risk of alienating some and under-utilizing the talents of others.

> **Quick Tip:** Don't talk about college with your employees. This is especially important if you are managing people older than you. The more you speak about how recently you went to college, the more it distances you from your employees and the more it makes them resent you or think that you are under-qualified and too inexperienced to be a manager.

Understanding Each Generation

Though it's important not to stereotype, effective managers must be aware of why certain generations view work and interact with others in the workplace the way they do. To help with that, here is a brief overview of each generation.

Baby Boomers

People of this generation, generally born between 1946 and 1964, grew up in turbulent times. The suburban family ideals of the 1950s transitioned to the birth of rock-n-roll and Woodstock, the

Vietnam War and the Civil Rights Movement, and the sense of fear caused by the Cold War. Amidst the chaos and turmoil, the Baby Boomer generation emerged as a strong and determined group, eager to express their sense of freedom and drive to succeed.

For this generation, work is important. It is the primary identifier of worth and the method of contributing to the world. Baby Boomers are driven by personal gratification, individual achievement, and accomplishment. To them, a good work ethic is important, and they tend to go further and push harder because of their own drive more than any pressure you put on them as a manager.

Baby Boomers are nearing the end of their careers. Due to the recent economic downturn, however, a significant portion of their retirement savings was lost, so they will most likely have to work longer than they originally anticipated. This may cause some frustration and a "one foot out the door" mentality, but hard work is ingrained in Baby Boomers, so they will still put forth notable effort to produce quality work. Moreover, many corporate executives fall into the Baby Boomer category.

Baby Boomers have varying levels of comfort with technology. They have adopted most new forms of communication and social networking (as seen in how our parents are on Facebook and have started texting), but they communicate differently than we do. Baby Boomers are more likely to prefer in-person or over-the-phone interactions to electronic forms of communication.

Many Baby Boomers will come across as inflexible with change, and it's important to manage their expectations. STAR managers find ways to leverage their depth of experience to benefit the entire team. Furthermore, Baby Boomers generally see Millennials as unprofessional and unmotivated. I was recently doing a radio interview and the host, a Boomer, went off about the lack of respect that Millennials have. A recent survey conducted by Workplace Options of American workers showed that 46 percent of employees believe Millennials are not engaged at work and 68 percent feel that Millennials are less motivated to take on responsibility and produce quality work. (See the full article, "Millennials Face Uphill Battle to Wow Co-Workers with Work Ethic," at *www.workplaceoptions.com/press-releases*.) This can create a higher hurdle for a Millennial manager. In addition to the possibility that Boomers may be upset about a "young kid" being their boss, they may assume that you are a slacker and that you will rely on *them* to do *your* work.

Generation X

Gen Xers, those typically born between 1965 and 1980, experienced a very different upbringing and have a different perception of work than their Baby Boomer elders. Gen X grew up with MTV, the public's exposure to the AIDS epidemic, the *Challenger* Space Shuttle explosion, and the fall of Communism.

While many Baby Boomers are accomplished and support the ideal of "manifest destiny," Gen Xers have become disenfranchised and maintain a skeptical approach to work. They were the first generation to experience widespread divorce, and grew up as "latch-key" kids, coming home to an empty house while their parents worked. This has made them self-reliant. This has also created a more important sense of family ahead of self as they strive to find balance.

Most members of Gen X are in the middle of their careers. They have families and kids, and look for a clear delineation between their work lives and home lives as they struggle to carve out time for their kids. Gen Xers have lower expectations and value practicality. At work, they don't want to do anything that isn't clearly defined or doesn't have a purpose.

Because they don't look up to inspirational figures, Gen Xers are generally not impressed by bosses, especially younger ones. By nature they question your authority, asking for justification as to why they need to follow your vision and goals. They see a job as only a job and do not tie as much of their worth to their work, instead counting friends and family as more valuable.

Members of Gen X echo many of the Baby Boomers' views of Millennials, skeptical of our work ethics, motivation, and engagement. Some of their viewpoints are more intensified when managed by a Millennial. Imagine how you would feel if your younger sibling was your boss!

Millennials

We have many labels, including Millennials, Gen Yers, the "Me" Generation, and the Trophy Generation. Whatever you call us, we are entering the workforce by the millions. Millennials are generally those born between 1981 and 2000 and have grown up with technology and an optimistic global mindset.

Because our parents are either Baby Boomers who felt guilty about how much they worked, or Gen Xers who don't want to replicate the empty households they grew up in, the world revolved around us. While Baby Boomers *proved* that they could do anything, we were *told* that we could do anything, so we wholeheartedly believe it. We feel that we *deserve* to be heard and will work hard for things we are passionate about.

We grew up in the age of the Internet, social media, and the 9/11 terrorist attacks. Instead of using traditional means to communicate and learn, we have embraced platforms of instant gratification, such as Facebook, Wikipedia, and YouTube. We believe in the interconnectivity of everything. Instead of a Gen-X cynicism and focus on family, Millennials focus elsewhere, embracing a sense of optimism and social impact.

We believe in multitasking to the Nth degree and have a much looser definition of what professionalism is and where the line between work and play falls. We are confident and are used to working in groups. We are polite to our bosses, and respect and value their role.

Although 47 percent of us say that we want to stay at the first company we work for out of school for five to 10 years (according to a study of the class of 2012 by Achievers and Experience Inc.), most of us lack the loyalty of older generations and believe that opportunity must be present to maintain our interest. (See the full article, "Achievers and Experience Inc. Reveal Class of 2012 Study Results to Understand the Needs of the Future Workforce," at *www.achievers.com/about-us/press-releases*.) In the book *Keeping the Millennials*, authors Dr. Joanne G. Sujansky, CSP, and Dr. Jan Ferri-Reed explain that our parents not only taught us to expect the best, but they also stressed that loyalty to a company does not pay.

Despite our enthusiasm and other positive traits, our parents have created a monster. Because we grew up believing the world revolves around us, we expect this to continue in the workplace, so we bring with us a sense of entitlement and impatience. We are very motivated about what we believe in, but at times lack the follow-through to see things to completion because our parents either cleaned up our messes for us or told us that it was okay to give up and that we shouldn't do anything we don't want to do.

Depending on the age of a Millennial, she may be in a career stage where she feels as though she can handle anything and that she will achieve anything and everything she wants, or she has reached that stage of disenfranchisement in which she realizes careers are hard and is desperately seeking the right path to the career her optimism expected.

> **Quick Tip:** Make it seem as though you are more experienced than you are. Talk vaguely about past experiences. Don't label your past experiences as internships when speaking about them. Don't share how long ago you did certain things because it reminds older employees how much younger you are than them. This is also true for your physical appearance. When I started out as a manager I changed my hairstyle and grew facial hair to look older, more experienced, and worthy of a management position.

How to Manage Each Generation

STAR managers translate all of this background information into actionable management practices in order to optimize the strengths of each generation. DOPE managers may understand the differences in their employees from each generation, but STAR managers actually adapt their style to create a healthy work environment for everyone.

Whereas each generation has its own complexities and nuances that must be considered to properly manage its members, there are a number of rules that apply when a Millennial manages any generation. Older employees will be skeptical of your abilities or authority, given your age and lack of experience, while Millennials will think that they are your friend, so it is important to balance your approach. Here are three keys to effective cross-generational management:

1. **Never pull the "I'm the boss" card.** It is a big mistake as a young manager to let authority go to your head. Instead of looking for ways to enact your power, let your direct reports know that you are there to help them, not boss them around. Offer them assistance in fulfilling their job responsibilities better and faster, and always do so with a helpful spirit.

2. **Ask their opinion.** This step is difficult and constantly overlooked. Remember that, at times, it is okay for your people to tell *you* what to do. When an older employee has a younger manager, the employee can feel threatened (think of Dennis Quaid's character in the movie *In Good Company*). Everyone has a desire to feel valued and that their opinion is important. When it comes to decisions that affect the team, get their input and do what you can to implement ideas they share. As John Baldoni says in the book *Lead by Example*, humility is an important skill of effective managers. Asking for input and admitting that you don't have all the answers is crucial for success. Great managers see their people as resources rather than threats.

3. **Explain the *why* behind things.** Baby Boomers have been around for a long time and don't want to be placated with lies or omission, Gen Xers are skeptical of any directives, and Millennials feel they deserve to know everything that you know, so it is important to explain *why* you are make the decisions you make. As a manager, you don't have an obligation to share these kinds of things with the team, but transparency goes a long way to developing trust when you

are a young manager. **Saying *"because I said so"* may work when you are a parent, but not when you are a boss.**

Baby Boomers

When managing a call center, I had a team of customer care representatives primarily made up of people who had been at the company longer than I had been alive. These Baby Boomers initially took the attitude that they would get their work done in order to not get in trouble, *in spite of* their young and inexperienced manager (me) instead of *because* of him. Young managers must earn the respect of Baby Boomers by being fair and giving them specific exposure to things that are going on behind the scenes. Asking for, and valuing, their opinions and advice is a great tool, not only for you to learn new strategies but for engaging them in their work. DOPE managers may write off their older employees as has-beens that just don't know "how things work" today, but STAR managers leverage older employees' experience to identify potential problems ahead and to learn best practices that can be adapted for today's working world.

You are better off having a face-to-face meeting or picking up the phone to converse with Baby Boomer employees instead of relying on e-mail or text. Reward Baby Boomers with financial benefits and the flexibility to take care of their aging parents. Because of their heads-down focus and work ethic, you may need to be more proactive about this instead of waiting for them to ask.

Gen X

STAR managers provide their Gen X employees with clear direction and deadlines. They allow their direct reports to determine the best way to fulfill their job responsibilities and reward them when they do. Recognize that by nature they will challenge your authority, so you must offer a balance between exerting your power and allowing them to have input.

In a number of positions where I managed Gen X employees, offering family time and a clearer separation between their work and personal life paid dividends. Respect their time when they are away from the office or on vacation. Be flexible for them and they will be more flexible for you.

Another best practice is to offer immediate perks and feedback to Gen Xers. Show them that you want to develop their skills, and align what they do with business goals so they can see how their role has a purpose for the greater organization and company. Additionally, although they are more comfortable than Baby Boomers with technology, Gen Xers value the personal relationship you create with them, so be willing to interact in person and take a genuine interest in aspects of their personal life; this will increase their engagement and level of motivation.

Millennials

Managing Millennials is a particularly challenging task. It may be easier to understand your Millennial employees, because you are one, but it is more difficult to assert your authority because, as mentioned, they may attempt to become informal with you, given the similarity in age. Resist interacting with them too much socially until you have an established relationship and track record of being their boss.

Motivate Millennial employees by allowing them to have work-life integration. Give them more freedom to have their own schedule and attempt to give them exposure to new and exciting things they are passionate about, all while treating each Millennial employee as unique and special. Pair them with more experienced employees so they can learn while also teaching older employees about technology.

As mentioned in *Keeping the Millennials*, establish and emphasize a respect for diversity, provide opportunities for advancement and reward, and engage and utilize your Millennial employees, because perks alone will not retain them for long. Be open to communicating via a variety of different platforms from instant messaging to text, and ensure that you are focusing your Millennial employees on the task at hand, or they will become distracted.

All in all, keeping it fun and offering benefits (including financial ones) while matching their career goals with the needs of the business will better engage Millennials.

☆ ☆ ☆

Whether your employees are "over the hill," reaching the peak, or just starting to climb, remember to be conscious of these generational differences and understand why your employees act the way they do in a professional environment. Adapt your style to create strong working relationships with all the generations and focus on creating a team culture to ensure each thrives.

> *The young man knows the rules, the old man knows the exceptions.*
>
> —Oliver Wendell Holmes

The STAR Manager vs. The DOPE Manager

The DOPE manager treats all employees the same, not taking advantage of the wisdom more experienced employees have. He maintains control and communicates in a way that makes sense to him, assuming that his employees will adapt accordingly.

The STAR manager values the strengths of employees of different generations. She adapts her style to create better relationships with older employees and those of her generation alike. She does not uphold an ego or desire to prove that she deserves to be a manager, despite her young age.

CHAPTER 17

You Can't Do It All By Yourself: Driving Results Through Others

What to Expect: Because managers are judged by the results of their team, this chapter discusses strategies that STAR managers perfect to lead through others, no matter what industry or business function the team is responsible for.

You're only going to be as good as your people's performance.

—Hal Leavitt

Effective leadership is not about making speeches or being liked; leadership is defined by results, not attributes.

—Peter Drucker

Managers who are fantastic motivators, inspiring visionaries, and wise coaches fall short of becoming STARs when they are not able to lead their teams to consistent solid results. All the excuses, best practices, and luck aside, effective management is about achieving results through others. This is why managers have a job. The methods may vary, but the outcome is always *results*.

This is where all of the elements used in building the second story to your house come together; starting with the house you built as an individual contributor, which becomes the foundation of your management structure. You then added on the second-story frame with management basics, such as workload balance and managing the competing interests of your boss and team. Finally, you created the exterior of the second story structure, built with the skills of STAR managers, including giving effective feedback, developing a team vision, motivating and empowering employees, and hiring the right people. All of this is for nothing without results.

Getting results is the determining factor for your personal career success, and the same is true for your role as a manager. As discussed in Book One of the Young Professional's series, *results are about substance*. Being a manager is not just what you do, how you do it, or how others perceive you; it is also about the results you lead others to achieve.

Getting results through others is about execution—executing on a plan and achieving goals. As Bossidy, Charan, and Burck say in *Execution: The Discipline of Getting Things Done*, execution is the discipline that is the main responsibility of a leader. It involves managing people, strategy, and operations, as well as rigor, depth, and intensity. To be effective you don't "sweat the details"; instead, you make execution a systematic process that starts with you. With execution placed at the center of your focus, the next step is to frame it with your *team-first* mentality.

In the final part of *The Young Professional's Guide to the Working World*, I outlined this equation for success:

SUCCESS = PASSION x SKILL

This same equation holds true for successfully driving results through others, and it brings together each of the key areas we've addressed in this book.

☆ **SKILL:** STAR managers build their team's skill level through hiring the right people and teaching them what they need to know to effectively on-board into their new position. Then, through coaching them, providing constructive feedback (tailored specifically to the individual, leveraging the contingency approach), and removing obstacles, they allow their employees to act more freely and be more conscious of the things they need to do to succeed.

☆ **PASSION:** STAR managers develop passion within their employees through establishing an inspiring vision and a healthy culture in an environment conducive to growth and success. They then gain their employees' trust and buy-in by removing obstacles, empowering them to take action and achieve goals while recognizing their accomplishments.

There is also a distinction to be made between good and bad results. A couple years ago, for example, a peer of mine's team chose to abuse a loophole they found in our compensation plan that allowed them to get paid twice for selling a similar product to the same customer. Results achieved through unethical means (bad results) should not be tolerated. It's important for you as a manager to step in with a strong hand to re-focus the team. Obstacles to reaching goals fairly will come up, but it is important to guide your team down a path where they can justly achieve goals. Then when these goals are achieved, ensure they are attained humbly. Do not boast. As John Wooden taught his players, after a game, someone who did not see the game should not be able to tell whether you won or lost from seeing you.

> **Quick Tip:** Make sure not to devalue accomplishing the little things. A number of little accomplishments directed at the right goal build up to big accomplishments. Habits also turn into results. Reward your employees' good habits.

How to Achieve Peak Performance Through Others

Besides the key enablers to driving results through others discussed thus far in the book (developing others, creating clear and simple goals that are tied to the employee's goals, and fostering accountability), the following are additional ingredients that drive your direct reports to achieve consistently high results.

☆ **Make them see the path ahead.** Some managers are effective at establishing the desired end state (a goal and vision) but are not able to show their team the steps needed to get there. STAR managers shed light on the path the team must take to achieve goals.

☆ **Make them believe they can do it.** People will achieve goals when they believe they can. On numerous occasions, I led teams to achieve improbable results because we all believed we could.

☆ **Take risks.** DOPE managers shy away from risk. When calculated, risks should be encouraged. STAR managers take the risk of moving as fast as they can, accepting failure as a valuable and educational side effect of risk that allows you to go faster and farther than if no risk was taken.

☆ **Keep an eye on results.** Results aren't the only thing, but they are probably the most important thing. Make sure your team stays on course by monitoring their performance. If you don't, then no one will. When you keep an eye out, not only do things get done, but you are also able to teach the team the right way to succeed and how to avoid failure, because you have visibility into each individual on your team, whereas they only have their own experiences.

☆ **Manage momentum.** Peak performance is intensified and perpetuated by momentum. STAR managers understand the importance of momentum. They work hard to prevent negative momentum when the team fails and, as in the curling example referenced in an earlier chapter, they pave the way for even more great results when the team starts doing well.

☆ **Follow through.** A STAR manager guides her team through the finish line. She knows when to push her team hard and when to empower them to achieve independently, using achieving her vision as a focal point.

☆ **Demand consistency.** STAR managers don't just drive results once; their results are sustainable. Be able to push the team hard when you really need to and help them consistently perform at a higher level.

Ensure that you leverage these ingredients to drive your team to exceptional results. Remember that when you uphold the basic management strategies and develop the other nine skills of young STAR managers, you will successfully guide your team to success.

Adopt a simple mindset: **Always give your best, and ask, inspire, expect, and remind your employees to do the same.**

Tell them that if at the end of the day they can look back at the effort they put forth, and know that they did their best, that is all you could ever ask of them.

Leaders who win the respect of others are the ones who deliver more than they promise, not the ones who promise more than they can deliver.
—Mark A. Clement

Well done is better than well said.
—Benjamin Franklin

The STAR Manager vs. The DOPE Manager

The DOPE manager shies away from risk, relying on comfortable methods to drive results. He doesn't mind the person and just focuses on the numbers, depreciating the passion of his employees.

The STAR manager knows that just as an individual contributor, as a manager her effectiveness will be judged by the results of her team. She actively elicits passion in her employees and develops their skills so they can succeed.

Explore Online: 10 Skills of STAR Managers Blueprint: On TheSparkSource.com, go to the Resources page to find a diagram and summary that details each of the 10 skills of the STAR manager.

PART III
Developing Into a STAR Manager

In this section, you will learn how to take the basic management traits and 10 skills of STAR managers and translate them into an effective management style. After reading, you will have a clearer understanding of the control you have over your unique management philosophy.

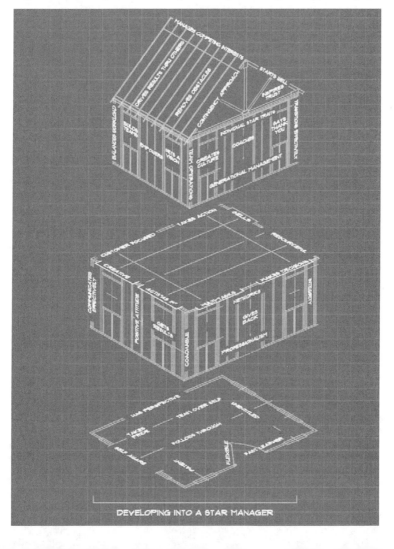

DEVELOPING INTO A STAR MANAGER

CHAPTER 18

The Manager's Blueprint: Building and Refining Your Management Style

What to Expect: This chapter details how to create a blueprint for becoming a successful young manager. It ties in important points and skills outlined in both Part 1 (Management Basics) and Part 2 (10 Skills of STAR Managers) and offers a pathway to action on the lessons you have learned.

If you're leading and nobody's following, you're just taking a walk.
—Chuck Smith

A desk is a dangerous place from which to view the world.
—John Le Carré

199

"...and those are my expectations of the team," I explained to my latest members, half of them new after another reorg.

"Now let me talk to you about my management style," I continued. "For those familiar with the Allstate Insurance logo, my management style adapts the logo into what I call 'Aaron's Allstate Hands.' Instead of two hands cupped in a semi-circle palms up, one hand stays below but the other pivots around back, so it looks more like a crocodile mouth or how a quarterback gets the football from the center."

"The hand behind pushes you forward, so we attain our best results. The hand below supports you. I know that if I push too hard, we will all fall off the edge," I said, my back hand pushing the imaginary item past the edge of the bottom hand and tumbling down. "But when I push and support at the same time," I exclaimed, pushing both hands in an upward fashion, "then together we will achieve more than we ever thought possible."

Corny? Yes. But also pretty effective. In fact, derivations of this style have worked across numerous job functions and with diverse groups of employees. When managing teams, it is most important that you formulate your own management strategy and accurately communicate it to your team.

Now that we have covered all the management basics and the 10 skills of STAR managers, it is time to focus on translating these concepts into action.

The first step is to develop your own unique management style.

As previously discussed, the contingency approach is an important element of all STAR managers' styles. The *situation* and the *people* involved will dictate the best derivative of your management strategy to act on. When crafting your management style, the one additional variable is You.

Each of us is different and therefore has unique strengths and weaknesses, comfort zones and styles. Some feel comfortable yelling at their team, using threats to get work done. Others don't have that capacity within themselves. Just as STAR individual contributors are self-aware, so are STAR managers. As a manager you will stretch yourself and routinely step out of your comfort zone, but it is important to understand the baseline of things you excel at and identify the things you struggle with.

Once you have these figured out (Book One of the series can help), you will understand the general demeanor and relationship you will naturally have with your team, adapting to fit the situation and people from there.

Despite individual uniqueness, a STAR manager's style has the 10 previously discussed skills and the following in common:

- ☆ **She is an effective delegator.** She inspects what she expects, knowing the team can accomplish more than she ever could on her own.

- ☆ **She sets clear expectations**, communicates them with her team, and upholds the standard she has set.

- ☆ **She is a decision-maker**, able to determine the right path forward despite competing interests and complex scenarios.

- ☆ **She is an advocate for her people,** supporting them when she believes they are right and giving them a voice with organization leadership.

- ☆ **She develops her employees**, ensuring they are constantly growing and that their careers are progressing.

- ☆ **She is fair, consistent, and follows through** on the commitments that she makes to her team.

- ☆ **She believes her people work *with* her and not *for* her.** She doesn't expect work to be done because she's "the boss." Instead she stands alongside her people to help them succeed.

- ☆ **She steps out of her comfort zone**, realizing that if she wants to stretch her team to grow and accomplish more, she must do the same herself.

- ☆ **She is committed to doing what is best for her team**, even when it involves more work for her or having to face a tough situation.

☆ **She has strong principles and values**, such as openness and honesty, from which she doesn't deviate, and that attitude permeates through the team's culture.

When you meld these characteristics with effective empowerment, creating the proper culture, developing trust and buy-in, providing appropriate recognition, coaching, and focusing on results, you can make any team unstoppable. Ensure that you understand and integrate these into your management style.

Elements of Your Management Style

A number of other variable elements are part of a a well-crafted management style. Think of each of the following dichotomies as a spectrum upon which you must find the right point, depending on the situation, the people involved, and yourself.

☆ **Separated vs. among the people.** It is important to have a good understanding of what the day-to-day is like for your employees (so you know what obstacles to remove), but it is important to have an outside perspective. Ensure that you step back when analyzing situations and choosing the best management tactics to use.

☆ **Following the plan vs. flexibility.** STAR managers use formal planning to create structure and focus the team. They are able to find the right balance between sticking to set plans and flexibly changing course when merited.

☆ **Authoritative vs. gathering input.** There will be times when it makes more sense to take a more autocratic role and other times when gathering thoughts from the team will make more sense in decision-making.

☆ **Research vs. intuition.** Some scenarios will merit a deep analysis and information gathering, whereas others will involve trusting your gut. STAR managers know when to trust their intuition.

☆ **Taking the lead vs. following.** Truly great leaders leverage the skills and talents of the group of smart people they build around them, and do so without needing to keep a tight grip on how goals are pursued and ultimately reached. They know when to take a leading role and when to let their employees lead the charge.

Crafting Your Management Style

When crafting your management style, it is important to conduct a personal inventory. This involves mapping out your strengths and weaknesses, and also taking note of the good and bad techniques you have experienced from other managers. The former will help you learn the areas where you need to develop and the latter allows you to study the right role models.

Next, test out various techniques in decision-making (autocratic, consensus-based, democratic) and find where your comfort zone lies. This, paired with your proper analysis of the situation and people (as outlined in Chapter 7), will offer clear structure around the right management tactics to implement.

Authors Zenger and Folkman reference a number of effective tactics in developing as a leader in their book *Extraordinary Leader*. The four most relevant to young managers are both straightforward and valuable:

1. Find a coach.
2. Connect with good role models.
3. Allocate specific time for people development.
4. Build personal dashboards to monitor leadership effectiveness.

Doing each of these on a regular basis helps you develop a strong management style and greatly increases your likelihood of success.

Putting Your Style into Action

Once you have developed a more concrete idea of the type of management style you want to enact, the next step is to build a formalized plan: your STAR Manager Blueprint. This plan, similar to the Career Blueprint in Book One, outlines how to effectively implement your management style and strategies. It also offers a step-by-step timeline on how to transition to a new management position.

Next, identify and build strong relationships with mentors to continuously develop as a manager.

You must then package and communicate your style to your employees. It doesn't have to be as goofy as "Aaron's Allstate Hands," but giving them some kind of reminder will help them understand your expectations and the type of relationship you strive for with your employees.

Remember that a STAR manager is consistent. She follows though with her team, upholding her chosen management style and expectations, guiding the team with the right approach, contingent on the situation and individuals involved.

So much of what we call management consists in making it difficult for people to work.
—Peter Drucker

The leader follows in front.
—Proverb

The STAR Manager vs. The DOPE Manager

The DOPE manager plays things by ear. He doesn't formally develop or communicate a set management style, leading him to be inconsistent with his reactions to situations and fostering a lack of follow-through. He relies on himself instead of others to craft his management style.

The STAR manager knows she has the ability to craft her own unique management style based on her skills and experience level. She proactively balances competing management tactics and maintains a mentality that she works *with* her employees instead of believing they work *for* her.

Explore Online: Go to TheSparkSource.com and look on the Resources page to find and fill out your STAR Manager Blueprint Templates.

CHAPTER 19

Managing Yourself: Continual Development and Improvement as a Manager

What to Expect: Becoming an effective young manager involves continuous development and is not just a level of understanding you reach once and maintain for the rest of your career. This chapter explains how to constantly monitor your development as a manager and leverage tools like mentorship and feedback to be consistently successful.

Always bear in mind that your own resolution to succeed is more important than any other.

—Abraham Lincoln

Effective managers live in the present but concentrate on the future.

—James L. Hayes

The STAR manager is constantly developing and growing. She understands the importance of building her management acumen, her familiarity with (and ability to appropriately perform in) a variety of different management positions, and she leverages resources to gain higher exposure opportunities with larger spans of control.

She proactively managers herself, monitoring her performance and progress, ensuring that she is aligned and balanced. She maintains a sense of empowerment and strives to reach her goals.

How to Build Your Management Acumen

To build your management acumen, STAR managers proactively look for challenging opportunities that are outside of their comfort zone. Instead of seeking the same scenarios (for example, always choosing a "turn-around" situation), they look to develop skills and experience in a variety of different circumstances.

At the same time, they focus on their strengths, just as STAR individual contributors do, to build a strong brand while mitigating career derailers. John C. Maxwell refers to this as getting "in the zone" and staying there, noting that effective leaders have certain "strength zones" and are most effective when they are invested in what they are best at.

STAR managers constantly monitor their progress. They leverage feedback mechanisms like 360-degree feedback, getting analysis of their strengths and weaknesses from their boss, peers, and employees alike. They find ways to measure their performance, but know that performance is not just measured in numerical results. STAR managers monitor the trust and buy-in they build within their team. They use resources like the "Customer Canvas" from Book One in the series, analyzing their employees as a customer.

As with STAR individual contributors, STAR managers don't fixate on *eliminating* all of their weaknesses. They instead focus on turning their best skills and attributes into their personal brand while *mitigating* career-harming shortcomings.

Moreover, effective managers practice. They realize that competent management involves taking risks as well as trial and error. As management guru Warren Bennis keenly points out, "Leaders learn by leading, especially in the face of obstacles where experience is transformed into wisdom."

STAR managers also realize that being a great manager is a process.

Time and time again, in our careers and lives in general, we make plans. We think through all the possibilities and details, noting as many variations as we can think of. Regardless of the planning or depth of analysis, we are often wrong. Things don't go as planned.

It is important for us to be patient when we embark on a journey to accomplish a goal, especially with a team in tow. As you drive down the road of your career, be sure to keep an eye out for delays. Often there won't be a sign that tells you when or why delays are coming. Remember not to let delays happen *to* you; use them to your advantage. Take away key lessons; they will help you be smarter and more successful farther down the road.

STAR managers, just like STAR individual contributors, listen to the world around them to see what they are doing right and what they are doing wrong. They take baby steps to break down large goals into smaller pieces. STAR managers leverage momentum to get even better results and uncover new opportunities, and take time to reflect so they can identify the best next steps.

Most importantly, STAR managers expect and embrace failure in both results and relationships with their employees, knowing that otherwise they aren't pushing hard enough.

Quick Tip: Find a mentor you connect with personally and then ensure he or she also aligns with your professional goals. Just because someone more experienced has accomplished something that you want to accomplish does not mean he is the best mentor for you. Ensure that you connect with him and that he is an effective motivator for you. When these things align, he will be more effective in mentoring you to achieve your goals.

The Importance of Mentoring for Managers

Mentoring is essential for all managers, even more than for individual contributors. There are so many more complexities and uncertainties in management roles than there were when all you had to do was care for yourself. STAR managers leverage mentoring to be more successful, knowing that they can't do it alone. STAR managers see mentors as the contractors who are helping them build the second-story additions to their career houses. Like contractors, these mentors know the right materials to use and how to construct effective management strategies.

Besides formal mentoring relationships, STAR managers use "mini mentors" who have expertise in a specific area that can help them better manage their team, whether it is in something company-related like a system or product, or more management acumen–related like effective recognition or delegation.

Finally, STAR managers use peer mentors, other managers who have had similar levels of experience and are of similar age, to bounce new ideas off of and to learn best practices.

Quick Tip: To ask for and receive advice on how to be an effective manager, leverage the PEER section of TheSparkSource.com. All posts are anonymous and are available for you to get advice whenever you need it, whether related to a large issue or a small question you have to help you solve a problem.

Above all, STAR managers ensure that they leave their mark on every organization they manage. Whether it be a specific success strategy or a lasting sense of empowerment, they leverage mentoring and self-analysis to make an impact. STAR managers focus on reinforcing their strengths to become better managers, while patiently growing amidst expected delays.

> *Self-development is a higher duty than self-sacrifice.*
> —Elizabeth Cady Stanton

> *Management is, above all, a practice where art, science, and craft meet.*
> —Henry Mintzberg

The STAR Manager vs. The DOPE Manager

The DOPE manager thinks that new management opportunities will come to him and that his rigid management style will ensure his success. He doesn't actively seek the guidance of others and pays too much attention to his weaknesses instead of turning his strengths into his personal brand.

The STAR manager realizes that being an effective manager is a continuous process. She regularly sharpens her skills, steps out of her comfort zone, and leverages mentors to learn how to be successful as she faces more complex high-pressure management situations with added responsibility.

Explore Online: Recommended Reading List: Check out the list of books recommended for all young managers on TheSparkSource.com Resources page.

PART IV
Finishing Touches

Having covered the keys to management success in this comprehensive guide, the book draws to a close with a reflection on what being a STAR manager truly is.

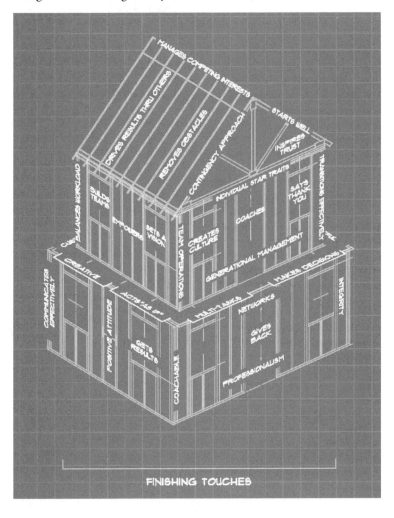

CONCLUSION

The STAR Manager in Action

We must remember that one determined person can make a significant difference, and that a small group of determined people can change the course of history.

—Sonia Johnson

As a manager, the important thing is not what happens when you are there, but what happens when you are not there.

—Ken Blanchard

The mediocre teacher tells. The good teacher explains. The superior teacher demonstrates. The great teacher inspires.

—William Arthur Ward

Imagine that you are on a hike. The sunrays peek through the trees as the lush foliage keeps you cool on a hot afternoon.

You have a ways to go until you reach your destination, but are confident, with the pace you are walking and the distance you have gone, that you will make your destination before dusk. Your map and GPS confirm this.

Behind you is the rest of group you are hiking with. Some are tired, some are sore from the miles traveled so far, but all are determined to reach the destination and enjoy an evening in the wilderness. This is a new trail for everyone, with many new sights and sounds, each bringing the group closer together as a cohesive unit.

Successfully guiding a group on a hike mimics the skills that STAR managers use to lead their teams.

As a hiking guide, similar to a manager, you set the pace. If you walk too fast, the group will spread out and some hikers will fall behind. If you travel too slowly, you will never reach your destination in time. When leading a hike, the guide must select a starting point and destination, identifying the appropriate path between the two, just as a manager identifies an end vision, helps her team see where they are today, and lays out steps and goals to make the vision a reality. For both roles, planning is key.

Just as managers have strategic plans they communicate to the team and use to illustrate progress made, a hike guide carries a map to keep track of how far down the trail the group is and shows the group the distance traveled. A great guide looks ahead, noting and sharing any changes in weather or terrain, just as a manager must anticipate change and improvise when it comes, keeping her team on the same page. At the same time, however, a manager must focus the team on the here and now so that mistakes aren't made that could take the team away from its goals, just the way a hike guide must keep an eye one step ahead on the trail to alert the team of any roots that could trip others up if they aren't watching their steps.

An effective hike guide will remove debris from the trail and will hold back branches so that the people behind won't get knocked off the trail, just as a STAR manager removes obstacles that hinder her team. Hike guides have a number of supplies from food to tools to keep the group going, just as managers use processes and initiatives to create momentum. The same way STAR managers assign roles to employees and efficiently delegate, hike guides give people different responsibilities, from tracking time to identifying the best lookout points.

Hike guides build in breaks so that people can reenergize and talk about the trail the group traveled on in the same way STAR managers take time to reflect on lessons learned with their teams. Recognition is essential for effective managers as they look for ways to thank their employees. Similarly, hike guides reward their hikers with beautiful views the group can enjoy at various points along the trail.

STAR managers know that the whole team must finish and that she is only as good as the poorest performer on the team. Hike guides similarly have to ensure the entire group completes the whole trail and no one gets left behind. Throughout the hiking process, good guides take time to let others lead the group, taking a turn walking among the group or pushing the team forward from behind. STAR managers find the same balance of leading and following their teams as well. Finally, hike guides do their best to make the experience fun, just as STAR managers build a healthy team culture where people enjoy coming to work.

Whether guiding a group down a trail or managing a team toward a goal, the skills are universal.

Besides the management basics and the 10 skills of STAR managers, which include balance, vision, motivation, recognition, empowerment, and being both a manager and a leader, there are *five additional things all STAR managers do* that are consistent throughout our comprehensive investigation of effective management.

1. **Make it about the team.** A STAR manager puts her team first, knowing that when her team achieves great things, so does she. Remember that sometimes the best way to learn how to lead is to learn how to follow.

2. **Set accurate expectations.** From day one, a STAR manager lets her team know what she expects and outlines the standards everyone must maintain. She then follows through to ensure everyone is living up to the established standards, pushing the team to improve.

3. **Leverage the contingency approach.** A STAR manager is consistent in principle yet adapts according to the situation, employees involved, and abilities she has developed.

4. **Treat people well.** A STAR manager knows that when you treat people well, they will work hard for you. She asks her people to put forth their best effort and knows they will give it to her if she inspires them.

5. **Drive results through others.** A STAR manager knows that success in business is more dependent on what you can get others to do than what you are capable of doing yourself.

Strive to make your people better and to leave a positive impact on every organization you are a part of, just as every STAR manager does.

At this point, you have built a sturdy house with a beautiful second-story addition. As you go forward in your career, be sure to maintain a certain level of upkeep and ensure that you fix any problems with your house. Strive to be a STAR, both on the upper level of your house as you manage others, and on the ground floor as you continue to develop yourself as an individual.

Remember, *good* managers lead their teams to amazing results when they are around, but *great* managers inspire outstanding results from their teams for years after they have moved on.

Index

About the Author

AARON MCDANIEL is a corporate manager, entrepreneur, author, and public speaker with a passion for helping Millennials build the foundation for successful careers. After graduating from UC Berkeley's Haas Undergraduate School of Business, Aaron entered the Leadership Development program at AT&T, a Fortune Global 100 company. After holding various management roles, Aaron became one of the youngest to serve as regional vice president.

Aaron is the founder of multiple ventures—one that successfully sold in 2012. His passion for helping young professionals succeed reaches back to his time at Haas, where he instructed the highly rated student-led course "Leadership and Organizational Dynamics" from 2002 to 2004, and continues through Spark Source, a "career incubator," and the first of its kind.

Outside of his professional life, Aaron is passionate about giving back through active community involvement in San Francisco, where he lives.